Extreme Hermeneutics Presents:

God Is Not Finished with Israel

A Comprehensive Biblical Study of the Covenants, the Church, and the Error of Replacement Theology

ISBN- 979-8-9958036-0-7

Disclaimer

This work is a theological study and reflects the author's interpretation of scripture. Readers are encouraged to examine the scriptures for themselves. "…they received the word with all readiness of mind, and searched the scriptures daily, whether those things were so" -Acts 17:11

Contact the Author: ExtremeHermeneutics@gmail.com

TABLE OF CONTENTS

INTRODUCTION

The Question That Must Be Answered

There are certain questions in scripture that do not remain isolated within a single doctrine. They extend beyond one topic and begin to shape how the entire biblical record is understood.

One of those questions is this:

Is God finished with Israel?

At first glance, this may appear to be a narrow theological issue—one that concerns only prophecy or the interpretation of certain passages. But upon closer examination, it becomes clear that this question reaches much deeper.

It touches:

- The nature of God's promises
- The consistency of scriptural language
- The relationship between the Old and New Testaments
- The structure of prophecy
- And ultimately, the reliability of God Himself

Why This Matters

If the promises made to Israel have been:

- Reassigned
- Redefined

- Or fulfilled in a way different from how they were originally given

Then a larger issue emerges:

Do God's words retain their original meaning?

If they do not, then:

- Language becomes flexible

- Interpretation becomes subjective

- And confidence in the certainty of scripture is weakened

On the other hand, if God's promises remain:

- Fixed

- Consistent

- And bound to the meaning in which they were spoken

Then those promises must be understood—and ultimately fulfilled—as they were given.

The Central Tension

Throughout history, many have concluded that Israel's role in God's plan has come to an end, and that the Church has taken its place. This perspective, commonly referred to as replacement theology, claims that:

- The Church is now the true Israel

- The promises to Israel are fulfilled spiritually

- National and covenantal distinctions no longer apply

At the same time, scripture continues to speak of:

- Israel as a nation

- Israel as God's people

- Israel as having a future

This creates a tension that cannot be ignored.

Either the language of scripture is being reinterpreted, or it is being taken as it stands.

The Method of This Study

This study does not begin with a theological system.

It does not begin with:

- Tradition

- Historical interpretation

- Or predetermined conclusions

Instead, it begins with a simple principle:

Let scripture define its own terms, establish its own categories, and interpret its own statements.

This means:

- Words are taken in their normal sense unless clearly redefined in the scripture itself

- Promises are examined in the context in which they are given according to scripture

- Patterns of fulfillment are allowed to establish interpretive consistency in the text

---

Each section of this study will examine a specific line of evidence:

- Covenants

- Identity

- Distinction

- Prophetic structure

- The character of God

Each of these lines will be followed independently of each other

And then, at the conclusion, they will be examined together.

The Expectation

If the lines of scripture evidence:

- Diverge

Then the conclusion must remain open to discussion.

But if they:

- Converge

Then the conclusion becomes unavoidable.

The Core Thesis

The argument presented in this study is not built on a single passage or a single idea. It is built on the cumulative weight of the entire scriptural record both in the old and new testaments.

And that argument is this:

God is not finished with Israel.

The promises made to Israel are:

- Unconditional in nature

- Grounded in the character of God

- Consistently affirmed throughout scripture

- And not yet fully realized

Therefore:

They must still be fulfilled as given and documented in the scripture.

A Final Word Before Beginning

This study is not written as a criticism of individuals, nor as an attempt to create division. Many great biblical scholars exist on both sides of the fence. We must remember that a true faith in the Lord and Savior Jesus Christ is what is of utmost importance. Scholars have disagreed throughout the centuries on many biblical topics.

It is written with a singular goal:

To examine whether the words of scripture mean what they say—and whether those words are allowed to stand on their own without reinterpretation.

If God speaks plainly, then the responsibility of the reader is not to reshape those words, but to understand them in the original intended context of the original author.

And if those words lead to a conclusion, then that conclusion must be accepted—even if it challenges long-held assumptions.

"The only barrier to truth is the presumption that you already have it." – Chuck Missler

The question, then, is not what has been traditionally believed.

The question is:

What does scripture actually say—and what happens when we allow it to speak for itself without the interpretations thought up by man?

From that point, the study begins.

PART I — THE FOUNDATION OF THE QUESTION

The Purpose of This Study

The purpose of this study is not to defend a theological system, nor to critique one from a position of preference. It is to examine a specific claim:

Has God permanently rejected Israel and transferred its promises to the Church?

This question is not secondary. It directly affects:

- How scripture is interpreted

- How God's character is understood

- How prophecy is applied

- How covenant language is defined

If God has redefined His promises after making them, then interpretation must follow that pattern. But if He has not, then any system that suggests otherwise must be carefully examined and refuted.

Defining Replacement Theology

Replacement theology (often called supersessionism) teaches that:

- The Church has replaced Israel in God's future plans

- The promises made to Israel are fulfilled in a spiritual sense through the Church

- National Israel no longer has a distinct prophetic future

This view does not typically deny scripture. Instead, it **reinterprets key terms**, including:

- "Israel"

- "Seed"

- "Land"

- "Kingdom"

Therefore, the central issue is not whether scripture speaks, but:

Whether the definitions given within scripture itself are allowed to remain consistent and true.

The Method of This Study

To avoid circular reasoning, this study will follow several fixed principles:

1. Terms will be defined by their consistent usage in scripture

A word will not be redefined in one passage unless the text clearly requires it. The definitions will not be changed to help strengthen a particular viewpoint or stance.

2. Promises will be interpreted in their original context

Covenants will be examined as they were given, not as they are later assumed to mean. Just because one assumes that a covenant meant something other than what was clearly given in the text does not make it so.

3. Literal statements will remain literal unless clearly symbolic

Symbolism will be recognized where the text indicates it—but not assumed where it does not. Scripture is very clear when symbols are being used. The bible uses over 200 forms of speech from puns to allegories. It always clearly defines when a form of speech is being used.

4. No single passage will carry the full argument

Instead, multiple independent lines of evidence will be developed. A single statement or passage is easily taken out of context.

5. Conclusions will be drawn only where those lines converge

This means the argument will not rest on:

- A single verse

- A single interpretation

- A single theological framework

The Central Question Restated

We are not asking:

- Are Gentiles included in salvation? (they clearly are and always were in the ultimate plan of God)

- Are believers united in Christ? (they clearly are according to Christ and the teachings of the New Testament writers)

We are asking something much more specific:

Do the promises made to national Israel still belong to Israel?

The Consequence of the Answer

This question carries weight beyond interpretation.

If God has permanently rejected Israel:

- Then unconditional promises have been altered

- Then "everlasting" does not mean everlasting

- Then original recipients can be reassigned

- God Himself would be a liar

But if He has not:

- Then Israel must still have a future role

- Then the covenants must still stand

- Then prophecy must still be fulfilled as given

- God shows Himself true to His word

Establishing the Starting Point

Before examining covenants, prophecy, or apostolic teaching, we begin with the simplest and most direct question scripture itself asks regarding this topic:

Romans 11:1

"Hath God cast away his people?"

The answer is immediate:

"God forbid."

Why This Matters as a Beginning Point

This is not:

- A debated conclusion

- A symbolic statement

- A complex theological construct

It is a **direct question with a direct answer and is giving no room for other interpretation**.

What Must Be Explained for replacement theology to be correct:

If replacement theology is correct, then this verse must mean something other than what it plainly states in the text.

Therefore, any system that claims Israel has been permanently replaced must explain the following:

- Why "God forbid" does not mean what it says

- Why "his people" no longer refers to Israel

- Why later passages in the same chapter describe a future for Israel

---

The Direction of This Study

From this starting point, we will examine:

1. The covenants made with Israel

2. The identity of Israel in scripture

3. The distinction between Israel and the Church

4. The present condition of Israel

5. The future restoration of Israel

6. The structure of prophecy, including Revelation

7. The arguments used to support replacement theology

Before asking how promises are fulfilled, we must determine **what was actually promised—and to whom**. Are these promises to a spiritual people? Are they simply to a single person? Did they include descendants? Did they include people that were not related to the people the covenants were given to?

PART II — THE ABRAHAMIC COVENANT

Why the Abrahamic Covenant Is Foundational

Before examining prophecy, Israel's future, or the role of the Church, we must begin with the covenant that establishes all of it.

The Abrahamic covenant is the root from which all subsequent promises grow from.

Every major theme that follows in scripture—land, nationhood, kingship, blessing to the nations—traces back to what God first declared to Abraham.

Therefore, if this covenant is:

- **Unconditional**

- **Not yet fully fulfilled**

then the conclusion is not optional or up for debate:

God is not finished with the people to whom this covenant was given.

The First Declaration of the Covenant

Genesis 12:1–3

"Now the Lord had said unto Abram, Get thee out of thy country, and from thy kindred, and from thy father's house, unto a land that I will shew thee: And I will make of thee a great nation, and I will bless thee, and make thy name great; and thou shalt be a blessing: And I will bless them that bless thee, and curse him that curseth thee: and in thee shall all families of the earth be blessed."

Observing the Structure of the Promise

The first and most important step is simply to observe what the text says in its original context.

God declares:

- "I will make of thee a great nation"
- "I will bless thee"
- "I will make thy name great"
- "In thee shall all families of the earth be blessed"

What is missing is just as important as what is present:

There are:

- No conditions stated
- No requirements listed
- No "if…then…" structure

God does not say:

"If you obey, I will…"

He says:

"I will…"

There were no conditions to be met on the part of Abraham.

So then the Initial Conclusion would be:

The covenant begins as a **divine declaration**, not a negotiated agreement.

The Introduction of the Land Promise

Genesis 12:7

"And the Lord appeared unto Abram, and said, Unto thy seed will I give this land: and there builded he an altar unto the Lord, who appeared unto him."

Observations from the Text

From this single verse, several things are clear:

1. The land is **promised by God and God alone**

2. The recipient is **"thy seed"**

3. The fulfillment is **future-oriented** ("will I give")

Important things to note:

The promise is:

- Specific

- Directed

- Not generalized

It is not given to:

- Humanity broadly

- A spiritual category

It is given to:

Abraham's seed and only to Abraham's seed

Expansion of the Promise

Genesis 13:14–17

"And the Lord said unto Abram, after that Lot was separated from him, Lift up now thine eyes, and look from the place where thou art northward, and southward, and eastward, and westward: For all the land which thou seest, to thee will I give it, and to thy seed for ever. And I will make thy seed as the dust of the earth: so that if a man can number the dust of the earth, then shall thy seed also be numbered. Arise, walk through the land in the length of it and in the breadth of it; for I will give it unto thee."

The Significance of "Forever"

This is the first time the duration of the promise is explicitly stated.

"To thee will I give it, and to thy seed **for ever**."

This raises a necessary question:

What does "forever" mean?

It cannot logically mean:

- A temporary possession that will be taken at a later date

- A symbolic inheritance only that has no actual value

- A promise later reassigned to another group

We can therefore conclude:

Any interpretation that removes the land from Abraham's descendants must first redefine the word:

"Forever"

The Formal Ratification of the Covenant

Genesis 15:9–12, 17–18

"And he said unto him, Take me an heifer of three years old, and a she goat of three years old, and a ram of three years old, and a turtledove, and a young pigeon. And he took unto him all these, and divided them in the midst, and laid each piece one against another: but the birds divided he not. And when the fowls came down upon the carcases, Abram drove them away. And when the sun was going down, a deep sleep fell upon Abram; and, lo, an horror of great darkness fell upon him. ... And it came to pass, that, when the sun went down, and it was dark, behold a smoking furnace, and a burning lamp that passed between those pieces. In the same day the Lord made a covenant with Abram, saying, Unto thy seed have I given this land, from the river of Egypt unto the great river, the river Euphrates:"

Understanding the Covenant Ceremony

To understand what is happening, we must recognize the cultural context.

In ancient covenant-making:

- Animals were divided into pieces

- Both parties would walk between the pieces

- This symbolized mutual obligation to one another

What Actually Happens

The text tells us:

- Abram is placed into a deep sleep

- He does not walk through the pieces therefore he does not oblige himself to keep his half of the covenant.

- God alone passes through (symbolized by the furnace and lamp)

This is the turning point:

Only one party binds Himself to the covenant.

The Nature of the Covenant Defined

Because God alone passes through:

The covenant is **unilateral**. Abram has not walked the path of the covenant and therefore has not agreed to uphold his end of the deal. God walks it alone after putting Abram into a deep sleep. God chooses to not have Abram walk the Covenant with Him.

Simply Meaning:

- Its fulfillment depends on **God alone**

- It is not dependent on Abraham's obedience

- It cannot be nullified by human failure

The Land Boundaries Defined

Genesis 15:18

"Unto thy seed have I given this land, from the river of Egypt unto the great river, the river Euphrates:"

Observations from the text

This is not symbolic language.

It defines:

- A starting boundary at a known location

- An ending boundary at a known location

- A real, geographic region known to the people

This brings us to a Critical Question:

Has Israel ever possessed this land:

- Completely?

- Permanently?

The answer is clear:

No.

The Everlasting Covenant Reaffirmed

Genesis 17:7–8

"And I will establish my covenant between me and thee and thy seed after thee in their generations for an everlasting covenant, to be a God unto thee, and to thy seed after thee. And I will give unto thee, and to thy seed after thee, the land wherein thou art a stranger, all the land of Canaan, for an everlasting possession; and I will be their God."

Two Elements That Cannot Be Separated

From this passage:

1. The covenant is **everlasting**

2. The land is part of that covenant

Therefore:

If the covenant remains, the land promise remains.

What Has Been Fulfilled

To remain precise, we must acknowledge:

- Abraham did become a great nation

- His descendants multiplied

- Blessing has come to the world through Jesus Christ

What Has Not Been Fulfilled

- The land has not been possessed in full as promised by God

- It has not been possessed permanently at this point in history

- The "everlasting possession" has not been realized

The Logical Conclusion

If the covenant is:

- Unconditional

- Everlasting

- Not fully fulfilled

Then:

Its fulfillment must still be future.

Final Thoughts on the covenant

The Abrahamic covenant stands as a unilateral, everlasting declaration made by God to Abraham and his descendants regardless of the actions of the people. Because its promises—particularly concerning land and permanence—have not yet been fully realized in history, they cannot be considered complete. Any system that asserts their fulfillment must do so by redefining the terms under which they were given. Scripture itself provides no indication that such redefinition has occurred. The covenant remains in effect, and its fulfillment remains future.

PART III — THE LAND COVENANT

(Restoration After Failure — Deuteronomy 30)

Why This Covenant Is Critical

After establishing that the Abrahamic covenant is:

- Unconditional

- Everlasting

- Not fully fulfilled

The next natural question arises:

What about Israel's disobedience then?

Did their failure:

- Cancel the promise?

- Transfer it to another people?

- Permanently remove them from the land?

The Context of the Covenant

Before examining the promise of restoration, we must understand the setting.

Deuteronomy 28

This chapter outlines:

- Blessings for obedience

- Curses for disobedience

It is important to note:

Israel's disobedience is not:

- Unexpected

- Hypothetical

It is **anticipated by God Himself in advance**.

The Scattering Is Predicted

Deuteronomy 28:64

"And the Lord shall scatter thee among all people, from the one end of the earth even unto the other…"

Key Observations:

- The scattering is global in scope

- It is severe

- It is presented as a consequence of disobedience against God

Key Point:

This is not the end of the story.

It is the setup for what follows.

The Turning Point — Restoration Promised

Deuteronomy 30:1–3

"And it shall come to pass, when all these things are come upon thee, the blessing and the curse… and thou shalt call them to mind among all the nations, whither the Lord thy God hath driven thee, And shalt return unto the Lord thy God… That then the Lord thy God will turn thy captivity, and have compassion upon thee, and will return and gather thee from all the nations, whither the Lord thy God hath scattered thee."

The Structure of the Promise

This passage outlines a clear sequence:

1. Israel experiences blessing and curse

2. Israel is scattered among the nations

3. Israel remembers

4. Israel returns to God

5. God regathers them

Critical Observation:

The restoration comes **after failure**, not instead of it.

The Scope of the Regathering

Deuteronomy 30:4–5

"If any of thine be driven out unto the outmost parts of heaven, from thence will the Lord thy God gather thee… And the Lord thy God will bring thee into the land which thy fathers possessed, and thou shalt possess it…"

Observations

- The regathering is:
    - **Global** ("outmost parts of heaven")
    - **Complete**
    - **Intentional**

- The destination is:

    o **The same land**

    o "Which thy fathers possessed"

This is critical to understand:

The land is not changed. The recipient is not changed.

The Nature of the Restoration

Deuteronomy 30:6

"And the Lord thy God will circumcise thine heart… to love the Lord thy God with all thine heart…"

What This Means for our study:

This is not merely:

- A political restoration

- A geographic return

It is also:

- **A spiritual transformation**

Important:

This transformation is **performed by God and God alone**.

The Order Matters

The sequence is:

1. Regathering

2. Restoration to the land

3. Heart transformation

This is significant because:

It shows that:

- Restoration is not dependent on prior perfection

- God brings them back **and then transforms them at a future time**

Has This Been Fulfilled?

To answer this, we must compare the text of scripture to actual history.

Has Israel been scattered globally?

Yes, as clearly accounted in history

Has Israel been regathered?

Partially (modern return). The regathering is still taking place today.

But has this happened fully?

Let's test the full criteria:

- Regathered from **all nations** (in process but not fully complete historically)

- Returned in **full obedience to God** (not yet)

- Heart transformation applied nationally (not yet)

- Permanent, secure possession of the land (not yet)

Conclusion:

This covenant has **not yet been fully fulfilled** but is being fulfilled as we write this paper

The Key Theological Implication

This covenant proves something important to understand and essential:

Israel's failure does not cancel their future promises.

Instead:

- Their failure leads to discipline by God

- Their discipline leads to scattering by God

- Their scattering leads to restoration ultimately by God

This Destroys a Core Replacement Argument

Replacement theology often claims:

"Israel lost the promises because of disobedience."

But this passage clearly shows:

- Disobedience was expected

- Scattering was predicted

- Restoration is guaranteed

Therefore we know:

Failure is not the end of the covenant.

It is part of the process that leads to its fulfillment.

Final Thoughts on This Section

The land covenant recorded in Deuteronomy 30 demonstrates that Israel's disobedience to God does not nullify the promises made to them, but instead initiates a process that ultimately leads to their restoration as promised throughout scripture. The scattering of Israel among the nations is not presented as a final judgment, but as a temporary condition as discipline followed by a guaranteed regathering, return to the land, and spiritual renewal. Because these elements have not yet been fully realized in history, the covenant remains active, and its fulfillment remains yet future.

PART IV — THE DAVIDIC COVENANT

(The Eternal Throne and Kingdom — 2 Samuel 7)

Why the Davidic Covenant Is Essential

The Abrahamic covenant established:

- A people named and called out by God

- A land promised to the people

- A promise of blessing upon the people

The Land Covenant clarified:

- Israel's failure does not cancel the promise of restoration

Now the Davidic covenant answers:

Who will rule over this people, in this land, under this promise?

The Setting of the Covenant

David desires to build a house for God.

Instead, God declares that He will build something for David:

A house—not of stone, but of dynasty.

The Covenant is Declared

2 Samuel 7:12–16

"And when thy days be fulfilled, and thou shalt sleep with thy fathers,
I will set up thy seed after thee, which shall proceed out of thy bowels,

and I will establish his kingdom. He shall build an house for my name, and I will stablish the throne of his kingdom for ever. I will be his father, and he shall be my son… And thine house and thy kingdom shall be established for ever before thee: thy throne shall be established for ever."

Observing the Structure of the Promise

From the text, several elements are clearly defined:

1. A **descendant of David** ("thy seed")

2. A **kingdom** that will be established

3. A **throne** that will endure

4. A duration described as **forever**

The Meaning of "Thy Seed"

"I will set up thy seed after thee, which shall proceed out of thy bowels…"

Observation:

This promise is:

- Biological

- Lineage-based

- Not symbolic

Therefore:

The promise is tied to: **A literal descendant of David**

The Nature of the Throne

"I will stablish the throne of his kingdom for ever."

Key question:

What is the "throne of David"?

From scripture, it is:

- A **real throne**

- Located in **Jerusalem**

- Connected to **Israel's national rule**

- Connected to **David**

Important:

Nothing in this passage suggests:

- A symbolic throne

- A heavenly-only throne

- A redefined spiritual authority

The Duration Given — "Forever"

This covenant repeats a key word:

"For ever"

As before, we must then ask:

Does "forever" mean:

- Temporary?

- Spiritualized?

- Reassigned?

- Symbolized?

The consistent scriptural answer must be:

No

The Relationship Between Discipline and Promise

2 Samuel 7:14–15

"If he commit iniquity, I will chasten him with the rod of men… But my mercy shall not depart away from him…"

Observations

- Discipline is expected
- Correction is applied
- But the covenant is **not revoked** or **broken**

This mirrors what we saw before:

Failure leads to:

- Discipline
- **Not** cancellation

Has This Covenant Been Fulfilled?

To answer this question, we must separate:

Partial fulfillment

from

Complete fulfillment

Partial Fulfillment:

- Solomon (David's son) sat on the physical throne of the kingdom

- A kingdom was established

But not complete:

- The throne has not endured continuously

- The kingdom is not currently established in its promised form

- The rule described as "forever" is not yet realized in history

---

The Role of Jesus Christ

Scripture identifies Christ as:

- The descendant of David

- The rightful heir to the throne

- The coming King

- He who Rules from Jerusalem

- One who's rule is eternal

Luke 1:32–33

"He shall be great, and shall be called the Son of the Highest: and the Lord God shall give unto him the throne of his father David: And he shall reign over the house of Jacob for ever; and of his kingdom there shall be no end."

Observations from This Passage of Scripture

- The throne is still called:

    - **"the throne of his father David"**

- The people are still:
  - **"the house of Jacob"**
- The reign is still:
  - **forever**

Critical Question:

Is Christ currently ruling:

- On David's throne
- Over the house of Jacob
- In the manner described here?

The answer is:

Not yet in this form.

The Location of the Throne

The throne of David is not described as:

- A heavenly abstraction
- A symbolic position or allegory

It is consistently tied to:

- Jerusalem
- Israel
- Earthly governance

Therefore:

If Christ fulfills this covenant fully:

His reign must be **real, visible, and located where the promise was given**

The Logical Conclusion

If the Davidic covenant is:

- Based on a literal descendant

- Connected to a real throne

- Described as everlasting

- Not yet fully realized

Then:

Its fulfillment must still be future.

The Theological Consequence

To maintain replacement theology, one must:

- Redefine the throne

- Redefine the kingdom

- Redefine the people being ruled

- Redefine the location of rule

But the text itself does not do this.

Final Thoughts on This Section

The Davidic covenant establishes an eternal throne, an enduring kingdom, and a perpetual line of rulership through the descendants of David. While this promise finds its ultimate fulfillment in Jesus Christ, the full realization of that reign—as described in scripture—has not yet occurred in history. The throne remains identified with David, the people remain identified as Israel, and the kingdom remains defined in terms consistent with its original declaration. Therefore, the covenant stands unfulfilled in its entirety, and its completion must still lie in the future.

PART V — THE NEW COVENANT

(National Transformation Promised — Jeremiah 31)

Why the New Covenant Is Essential

The previous covenants established:

- A people (Abrahamic)

- A land and restoration after failure (Land Covenant)

- A king and eternal throne (Davidic)

The New Covenant answers the final piece:

How will Israel be brought into full obedience and relationship with God?

The Covenant Declared

Jeremiah 31:31–33

"Behold, the days come, saith the Lord, that I will make a new covenant with the house of Israel, and with the house of Judah: Not according to the covenant that I made with their fathers… which my covenant they brake… But this shall be the covenant that I will make with the house of Israel; After those days, saith the Lord, I will put my law in their inward parts, and write it in their hearts; and will be their God, and they shall be my people."

Identifying the Recipients

The text is explicit:

"With the house of Israel, and with the house of Judah"

Observations:

- Two specific groups are named
- These are:
  - Historical Kingdoms
  - National People
  - Ethnic identities

Important:

The text does not say:

- "With all believers"
- "With the Church"
- "With a redefined Israel"

The Contrast with the Old Covenant

"Not according to the covenant… which they brake…"

Meaning:

- The Mosaic covenant was:
  - Conditional
  - Broken by Israel
- The New Covenant is:
  - Not based on that structure
  - Designed to overcome that failure and be unbreakable

This connects directly to what we've already seen:

Israel's failure does not end the story or the covenant promise. It leads to a new form of restoration

---

The Nature of the Transformation

Jeremiah 31:33

"I will put my law in their inward parts, and write it in their hearts…"

Observations

This is:

- Internal, not external

- Transformational, not instructional

- Divine in origin, not human effort

Key point:

God does not command obedience— He **creates it within them**. This is a spiritual and supernatural change.

The Scope of the Covenant

Jeremiah 31:34

"And they shall teach no more every man his neighbour… saying, Know the Lord: for they shall all know me, from the least of them unto the greatest of them…"

Observations

- This describes:

    - Universal knowledge of God within the group

- Not partial

- Not limited

This is crucial:

It is not describing:

- A mixed condition

- A partially obedient people

It describes:

A fully transformed nation

The Issue of Forgiveness

"For I will forgive their iniquity, and I will remember their sin no more."

This is:

- Complete forgiveness

- Final

- Irreversible

The Permanence of Israel Reinforced

Immediately after describing the New Covenant, God makes an extraordinary statement:

Jeremiah 31:35–37

"Thus saith the Lord, which giveth the sun for a light by day… If those ordinances depart from before me… then the seed of Israel also shall cease from being a nation before me for ever. …If heaven above can be measured… I will also cast off all the seed of Israel…"

Observations

God ties Israel's existence to:

- The sun

- The moon

- The stars

- The structure of the very creation itself

Meaning:

Israel's identity as a nation is:

As stable as the created order of all things

Has This Covenant Been Fulfilled?

We must test this carefully.

Are individuals experiencing New Covenant blessings?

Yes (through faith in Jesus Christ) on a personal and individual level

But has this happened nationally?

Let's apply the criteria:

- All Israel knows the Lord (not yet)

- Full internal transformation (not yet)

- Complete national obedience (not yet)

- Universal participation within the nation (not yet)

Conclusion:

The covenant is:

- **Initiated**

- But not **fully realized nationally** at this point in history

---

The Relationship to the Church

This is where confusion often arises.

Believers today:

- Participate in the **spiritual blessings** of the New Covenant

But that does not mean:

- The original recipients have been replaced

Important distinction:

Participation does not equal the transfer of identity

The Logical Conclusion would then be

If the New Covenant is:

- Made explicitly with Israel and Judah

- Describing a complete national transformation

- Not yet fully realized

Then:

Its full fulfillment must still be future—and must involve national Israel.

The Theological Consequence

To maintain replacement theology then, one must:

- Redefine "Israel and Judah"

- Redefine "nation"

- Redefine "all shall know me"

But again:

The text itself does not do this.

Final Thoughts on This Section

The New Covenant, as declared in Jeremiah 31, is explicitly made with the house of Israel and the house of Judah and promises a complete internal transformation, universal knowledge of God, and total forgiveness of sin within that nation. While believers today experience aspects of this covenant through Christ, its full national realization has not yet occurred. Because the covenant includes elements that remain unfulfilled, it cannot be considered complete, and its fulfillment must still lie in the future. Israel therefore, remains central to the unfolding of God's redemptive plan as plainly stated in scripture.

MAJOR MILESTONE

At this point, we have fully established the four core covenants.

1. Abrahamic — People, land, promise

2. Land Covenant — Restoration after failure

3. Davidic — Eternal throne and kingdom

4. New Covenant — National transformation

And all four are:

- Unconditional
- Not fully fulfilled
- Still pointing forward toward the future

PART VI — THE IDENTITY OF ISRAEL IN SCRIPTURE

Why This Question Is Essential

Up to this point, we have established:

- God made covenants with Israel as a people

- Those covenants are unconditional and to break them would make God a liar

- Those covenants are not yet fully fulfilled

At this stage, the only way to avoid the conclusion that Israel still has a future is to redefine the term:

"Israel"

The question then becomes:

Does scripture itself ever redefine "Israel" to mean:

- The Church?

- A spiritual collective?

- All believers regardless of lineage?

Or does it consistently maintain its original meaning?

The Original Definition of Israel

The term "Israel" originates with a specific individual.

Genesis 32:28

"Thy name shall be called no more Jacob, but Israel…"

Observations

- "Israel" is first a **person**
- Then becomes:
    - A **family**
    - A **nation**
    - A **people group descended from Jacob** with unique promises from God

Important:

The definition is:

- Historical
- Genealogical
- National

Consistent Old Testament Usage

Throughout the Old Testament:

"Israel" refers to:

- Jacob himself
- The descendants of Jacob
- The nation formed from those descendants

Examples include:

- National blessings
- National judgment
- National restoration

There is no instance where:

"Israel" is redefined to mean:

- Gentiles or any other people that are not a direct descendant of Jacob

- A spiritualized group detached from lineage

The New Testament Usage Must Also Be Tested

If a redefinition exists, it must occur in the New Testament.

The key question:

Does the New Testament redefine "Israel," or does it continue using it in the same way?

Paul's Use of "Israel"

The clearest test case is found in:

Romans 9–11

Example:

Romans 11:1

"Hath God cast away his people? God forbid. For I also am an Israelite…"

Observations

Paul identifies himself as:

An Israelite

This is:

- Ethnic

- Lineage-based

- Not symbolic

Therefore:

"Israel" still refers to:

A definable people group that were know to the people at his time of writing

---

The Distinction Between Israel and Gentiles

Romans 11:25

"Blindness in part is happened to Israel, until the fullness of the Gentiles be come in."

Observations

This verse clearly distinguishes:

- Israel

- Gentiles

- The co-existence of the two during the same time period

Logical necessity:

If "Israel" = Church

Then "Gentiles" = Church

Result:

The distinction collapses into contradiction.

Therefore:

"Israel" cannot mean the Church in this context.

The Olive Tree Illustration

Romans 11:17–24

17 And if some of the branches be broken off, and thou, being a wild olive tree, wert graffed in among them, and with them partakest of the root and fatness of the olive tree;

18 Boast not against the branches. But if thou boast, thou bearest not the root, but the root thee.

19 Thou wilt say then, The branches were broken off, that I might be graffed in.

20 Well; because of unbelief they were broken off, and thou standest by faith. Be not highminded, but fear:

21 For if God spared not the natural branches, take heed lest he also spare not thee.

22 Behold therefore the goodness and severity of God: on them which fell, severity; but toward thee, goodness, if thou continue in his goodness: otherwise thou also shalt be cut off.

23 And they also, if they abide not still in unbelief, shall be graffed in: for God is able to graff them in again.

24 For if thou wert cut out of the olive tree which is wild by nature, and wert graffed contrary to nature into a good olive tree: how much more shall these, which be the natural branches, be graffed into their own olive tree?

Paul describes:

- Natural branches (Israel)

- Wild branches (Gentiles)

- One tree (covenant structure)

Observations

- Israel is not replaced
- Israel is partially removed for a purpose
- Gentiles are added

Key statement:

God can:

"graft them in again"

Meaning:

- Israel retains identity
- Restoration is possible
- Replacement has not occurred

The Meaning of "All Israel"

Romans 11:26

"And so all Israel shall be saved…"

Observations

- "Israel" has been consistently defined throughout the chapter
- No redefinition is introduced here

Therefore:

"All Israel" must refer to:

The same Israel discussed throughout the entire passage

The Argument from Consistency

If "Israel" means:

- Ethnic Israel in verse 1

- Ethnic Israel in verse 25

Then it must also mean:

- Ethnic Israel in verse 26

Otherwise:

The passage becomes internally inconsistent.

The Only Common Counterexample

The primary passage used to argue redefinition is:

Galatians 6:16

"Peace be on them… and upon the Israel of God."

Observations

This verse:

- Does not define the term

- Does not explicitly equate Israel with the Church

Grammatically, it can refer to:

- Believing Jews within the broader group

Critical point:

A single ambiguous verse cannot overturn:

- Consistent usage across all scripture

The Absence of Explicit Redefinition

Now we ask a direct question:

Where does scripture clearly state that "Israel" now means the Church?

The answer:

It does not.

This is decisive:

A concept this significant would require:

- Clear explanation from scripture itself

- Direct teaching from Jesus or one of the apostles

- Repeated clarification throughout scripture

However, when we look through scripture, **none exists.**

The Logical Conclusion

If:

- "Israel" is consistently defined throughout the complete bible

- That definition is never explicitly changed or altered

- That definition is required for covenant interpretation and meaningful promises

Then:

Israel must still mean Israel.

The Theological Consequence

If Israel is not redefined, then:

- The covenants still apply to Israel as a people and nation

- The promises still belong to Israel

- The future restoration still involves Israel

Final Thoughts on This Section

The term "Israel," as used throughout scripture, maintains a consistent meaning rooted in the descendants of Jacob as a distinct, identifiable people group and nation. Neither the Old Testament nor the New Testament provides a clear or explicit redefinition of this term to include the Church or to exclude its original referent. While believers from all nations are brought into spiritual unity through Christ Jesus, this unity does not erase or abolish the distinctions clearly established by God in His covenantal dealings with His covenant people. Therefore, the identity of Israel remains intact, and the promises made to Israel remain applicable to that same people and nation.

PART VII — THE DISTINCTION BETWEEN ISRAEL AND THE CHURCH

Why This Distinction Matters

At this stage, the argument has established:

- The covenants remain in effect

- Israel's identity has not been redefined

The remaining question is:

Are Israel and the Church the same entity, or are they distinct within God's ultimate plan?

If they are the same entity:

- The promises to Israel may be reassigned

If they are distinct from each other:

- The promises to Israel must remain with Israel

A Direct Threefold Distinction in Scripture

1 Corinthians 10:32

"Give none offence, neither to the Jews, nor to the Gentiles, nor to the church of God:"

Observations from the Text

This verse identifies three separate groups:

1. **The Jews**

2. **The Gentiles**

3. **The Church of God**

Logical Implication

These are not overlapping categories in this statement.

They are presented as:

- Distinct groups of people

- Recognizable

- Existing simultaneously

Critical Point

If the Church were identical to Israel, this verse would collapse into redundancy.

It would read:

- Jews

- Gentiles

- Jews

Which is logically inconsistent and makes no sense.

Therefore:

The Church is not the same as Israel.

The Future Nature of the Church

Matthew 16:18

"And I say also unto thee, That thou art Peter, and upon this rock I will build my church; and the gates of hell shall not prevail against it."

Observations

- Christ speaks of the Church as something He **"will build"** in the future tense

- This indicates:

    o The Church is **future** at this point

    o It is not already established as Israel

Conclusion

The Church is:

- Not identical to Israel

- Not a continuation of Israel in its original form both as a people and a nation

---

The Formation of the Church

Acts 2:1–4

"And when the day of Pentecost was fully come, they were all with one accord in one place. And suddenly there came a sound from heaven as of a rushing mighty wind… And they were all filled with the Holy Ghost…"

Observations

- The Church is formed through:

    o The coming of the Holy Spirit indwelling in the individual

- This marks:

    o A new phase

    o A new structure

Important

This is not:

- The continuation of national Israel

It is:

The formation of a new body

The Nature of This New Body

Ephesians 2:14–16

"For he is our peace, who hath made both one, and hath broken down the middle wall of partition between us; Having abolished in his flesh the enmity… For to make in himself of twain one new man, so making peace; And that he might reconcile both unto God in one body by the cross…"

Observations from the Text

- Two groups are identified:
  - Jews
  - Gentiles
- These two are brought together into:
  - **"One new man"**
  - **"One body"**

Critical Insight

The text does not say:

- Jews become Gentiles
- Gentiles become Jews

It says:

They become something new in Christ. This means those outside of Christ would still retain their identities and nationality.

Therefore:

The Church is not:

- Israel expanded

It is:

A distinct entity formed from both groups in Christ

Unity Does Not Eliminate Distinction

The Church is unified in Christ.

However, unity does not mean:

- Erasure of identity
- Cancellation of prior promises

This principle is already demonstrated in the text:

Two groups remain identifiable even as they are unified.

Example:

A family may be unified, but members still retain individual identity. The father does not become the mother. The father stays the father and the mother stays the mother. Together however they are a single family unit.

The Olive Tree Illustration

Romans 11:17–18

"And if some of the branches be broken off, and thou, being a wild olive tree, wert grafted in among them… Boast not against the branches…"

Observations

- Natural branches = Israel

- Wild branches = Gentiles

- Gentiles are:

    o **Grafted in**

    o Not replacing the root

    o Not naturalized

Key Point

The original branches are not destroyed.

They are:

- Broken off temporarily

- Capable of being restored

The Possibility of Restoration

Romans 11:23–24

"And they also, if they abide not still in unbelief, shall be grafted in: for God is able to graft them in again."

Observations

- Israel can be:
  - Restored
  - Reinserted into the same structure
  - Remain unique in identity

This proves:

- Israel retains identity and uniqueness
- Israel retains its place in God's plan
- Israel is not replaced by the Gentiles

The Warning Against Replacement Thinking

Romans 11:18

"Boast not against the branches…"

Meaning

Gentiles are warned:

- Not to assume superiority
- Not to assume permanence of position
- Not to assume replacement

Why?

Because:

- The original branches still belong
- The structure still includes them

Summary of the Distinction

From the passages examined:

- Israel remains:
    - A distinct, covenantal people
- The Church is:
    - A new body formed in Christ including both Jews and Gentiles
- Both:
    - Exist within God's plan
    - Are not identical

Category	Israel	Church
Origin	Abrahamic lineage	Formed in Christ
Basis	Covenant nation	Spiritual body
Composition	Ethnic descendants	Jew + Gentile
Promises	Land, nation, kingdom	Spiritual blessings
Role	National & prophetic	Spiritual & corporate

The Logical Conclusion

If:

- Scripture distinguishes Israel from the Church
- Scripture shows both existing simultaneously and uniquely
- Scripture describes the Church as a new entity including both

Then:

The Church cannot be a replacement for Israel.

The Theological Consequence

Replacement theology requires:

- Merging these identities
- Reassigning promises
- Ignoring distinctions

But scripture maintains:

- Distinction
- Order
- Continuity

Another example in Scripture

Galatians 3:28 (KJV)

"There is neither Jew nor Greek, there is neither bond nor free, **there is neither male nor female**: for ye are all one in Christ Jesus."

Observations:

In this verse concerning the oneness in Christ there are two more added categories totaling three

- Bond and Free
- Male and Female
- Jews and Gentiles

To argue that Jews and Gentiles loose their identities outside of Christ, one would also have to argue:

- Bond and free loose their identities outside of the church

- Males and Females loose their identities outside of the church

Clearly this is not the case

Final Thoughts on This Section

The New Testament consistently maintains a distinction between Israel and the Church the same way it maintains a distinction between men and women. While both participate in God's redemptive work through Christ, they are not presented as the same entity nor do they have the same role. Israel remains a covenantal nation defined by descent and promise, while the Church is a new body formed through the uniting of Jews and Gentiles in Christ. Because these identities are not merged in scripture, the idea that the Church replaces Israel is not supported by the text.

PART VIII — ISRAEL'S PRESENT CONDITION

(Partial Hardening and Its Purpose — Romans 11)

The Question Scripture Itself Asks

Romans 11:1

"I say then, Hath God cast away his people? God forbid. For I also am an Israelite, of the seed of Abraham, of the tribe of Benjamin."

Observations

- The question is direct:

    o   Has God rejected Israel?

- The answer is immediate and concise:

    o   "God forbid"

- Paul supports this by identifying himself as:

    o   An Israelite

    o   A descendant of Abraham

Conclusion

Israel's current condition cannot be explained as:

Total rejection

The Concept of a Remnant

Romans 11:5

"Even so then at this present time also there is a remnant according to the election of grace."

Observations

- Even in unbelief, a portion of Israel:
  - Believes
  - Is saved

Meaning

Israel is not:

- Entirely rejected
- Entirely cut off

There is:

A preserved remnant

The Hardening Described

Romans 11:7–8

"What then? Israel hath not obtained that which he seeketh for; but the election hath obtained it, and the rest were blinded. (According as it is written, God hath given them the spirit of slumber, eyes that they should not see…)"

Observations

- There are two groups within Israel:

    1. The elect (believing remnant)

    2. The rest (hardened)

Important

This is:

- Partial

- Not total

The Purpose of Israel's Stumbling

Romans 11:11

"I say then, Have they stumbled that they should fall? God forbid: but rather through their fall salvation is come unto the Gentiles, for to provoke them to jealousy."

Observations

- Israel's stumbling is not:

    o Final

    o Permanent

- It has a purpose:

    o Salvation goes to Gentiles

    o Israel is provoked to jealousy

Conclusion

Their fall is:

Instrumental, not terminal

The Temporary Nature of the Hardening

Romans 11:25

"For I would not, brethren, that ye should be ignorant of this mystery… that blindness in part is happened to Israel, until the fullness of the Gentiles be come in."

Observations

This verse defines the hardening in three ways:

1. **Blindness in part** → Not total

2. **Happened to Israel** → Still referring to Israel

3. **Until** → Temporary status

The word "until" is decisive

It establishes:

A defined endpoint

What Happens After the "Until"

Romans 11:26

"And so all Israel shall be saved: as it is written, There shall come out of Sion the Deliverer…"

Observations

- This follows directly after the "until"
- It describes:
    - A future salvation and deliverance of Israel

Important

"All Israel" must refer to:

- The same Israel discussed throughout the entire chapter

The Covenant Connection

Romans 11:27

"For this is my covenant unto them, when I shall take away their sins."

Observations

- Israel's future salvation is tied to:
    - Covenant promises and God's unique power
- This connects directly to:
    - The New Covenant

Meaning

The future restoration is not:

- A new idea
- A replacement plan

It is:

The fulfillment of existing covenants

Israel's Status Summarized

Romans 11:28

"As concerning the gospel, they are enemies for your sakes: but as touching the election, they are beloved for the fathers' sakes."

Observations

Israel is described in two ways:

1. **Enemies (present condition)**

2. **Beloved (covenant status)**

This is critical to understand

Their present rejection does not cancel:

Their covenant identity

The Irrevocable Nature of God's Calling

Romans 11:29

"For the gifts and calling of God are without repentance."

Observations

- God does not:

  o Revoke his gifts

  o Withdraw his presence

  o Change His promises

Therefore

What was given to Israel:

Remains in effect

The Logical Structure of This Chapter

When taken together, Romans 11 teaches:

- Israel is not rejected

- Israel is partially hardened

- The hardening is a temporary condition

- The hardening serves a purpose outside of their own

- Israel will be restored in the future

The Logical Conclusion

If:

- Israel is only partially hardened

- That hardening has an endpoint

- Their future salvation is guaranteed

- Their covenant status remains

Then:

Israel's current unbelief is a temporary state, not final

Final Thoughts on This Section

Romans 11 provides a direct and systematic explanation of Israel's present condition. The nation is not described as rejected, but as partially hardened. This hardening is temporary, purposeful, and bounded by a defined endpoint, after which Israel will experience national restoration and salvation. Their present state, therefore, cannot be interpreted as evidence of replacement, but must instead be understood as a transitional phase within the larger framework of God's covenantal plan.

PART IX — THE FUTURE RESTORATION OF ISRAEL

(Prophetic Convergence — National Repentance, Regathering, and Kingdom)

Why This Section Is Necessary

If Israel:

- Is not rejected

- Is only temporarily hardened

Then scripture must describe:

What happens next

This section will demonstrate that the future of Israel includes:

- National repentance

- Spiritual transformation

- Physical regathering

- A restored kingdom

- The reign of Jesus Christ

National Repentance Foretold

Zechariah 12:10

"And I will pour upon the house of David, and upon the inhabitants of Jerusalem, the spirit of grace and of supplications: and they shall look upon me whom they have pierced, and they shall mourn for him, as one mourneth for his only son…"

Observations

- The recipients are:
    - "The house of David"
    - "The inhabitants of Jerusalem"
- The response is:
    - Mourning
    - Recognition
    - Repentance

Critical Insight

This is not:

- Individual conversion scattered across history

It is:

A national event with a national people

The Cleansing That Follows

Zechariah 13:1

"In that day there shall be a fountain opened to the house of David and to the inhabitants of Jerusalem for sin and for uncleanness."

Observations

- The phrase "in that day" connects directly to the repentance in chapter 12

- The cleansing is:
    - Immediate
    - National
    - Complete

Meaning

Repentance leads directly to:

Spiritual restoration

The Regathering of Israel

Ezekiel 36:24–26

"For I will take you from among the heathen, and gather you out of all countries, and will bring you into your own land. Then will I sprinkle clean water upon you, and ye shall be clean… A new heart also will I give you…"

Observations

The sequence is clear:

1. Regathering from the nations
2. Return to the land that is **Their Land**
3. Spiritual cleansing
4. Heart transformation

Important

This mirrors what we saw in:

- Deuteronomy 30
- The New Covenant

The Valley of Dry Bones (National Restoration)

Ezekiel 37:11–14

"Son of man, these bones are the whole house of Israel... Behold, I will open your graves... and bring you into the land of Israel...
And shall put my spirit in you, and ye shall live..."

Observations

- The interpretation is given:
  - "The whole house of Israel"
- The restoration includes:
  - Physical reassembly in the land of Israel
  - Spiritual life

Meaning

This is:

National resurrection and restoration

The Kingdom Restored

Isaiah 2:2–3

"And it shall come to pass in the last days... the mountain of the Lord's house shall be established... and all nations shall flow unto it... For out of Zion shall go forth the law, and the word of the Lord from Jerusalem."

Observations

- Location:
    - Jerusalem
- Participants:
    - All nations of the world
- Authority:
    - The Lord ruling from Zion

This is:

- Geographic in context
- Visible to the people of the world
- Global in scope

The Reign of the Lord from Jerusalem

Zechariah 14:4, 9

"And his feet shall stand in that day upon the mount of Olives…
And the Lord shall be king over all the earth…"

Observations

- The return is:
    - Physical
    - Located
    - Visible
- The reign is:
    - Global

- o Centered in Israel

This fulfills:

- The Davidic covenant
- The kingdom promises

Jesus Confirms a Future Turning Point

Matthew 23:37–39

"O Jerusalem, Jerusalem… Ye shall not see me henceforth, till ye shall say, Blessed is he that cometh in the name of the Lord."

Observations

- Jesus addresses:
  - o Jerusalem
- He states:
  - o A future moment of recognition when they acknowledge Him as Lord

Key word:

"Till"

Meaning:

- Their rejection is not final
- Their acceptance is future

The Disciples' Expectation

Acts 1:6–7

"Lord, wilt thou at this time restore again the kingdom to Israel? And he said unto them, It is not for you to know the times…"

Observations

- The disciples expect:
    - A restored literal kingdom
    - For Israel
- Jesus does not correct:
    - The expectation of a restored kingdom

He corrects:

- The timing of the restoration

Meaning

The concept of:

A restored kingdom to Israel is affirmed

The Convergence of Prophecy

When these passages are placed together, a consistent pattern emerges:

1. Israel is regathered

2. Israel repents

3. Israel is cleansed

4. Israel is spiritually transformed

5. Christ returns

6. Christ reigns from Jerusalem

7. The nations are governed from Israel

What Has Not Yet Happened

To remain precise:

- Israel has not yet experienced national repentance

- Israel has not yet undergone full spiritual transformation

- Christ is not yet reigning from Jerusalem

- The nations are not yet flowing to Zion in this manner

Therefore:

These prophecies remain:

Future

The Logical Conclusion

If:

- The prophets describe a future national restoration

- Jesus confirms a future turning point

- The apostles expect a restored kingdom

Then:

Israel's future is not symbolic—it is literal and still to come

Final Thoughts on This Section

The prophetic scriptures consistently describe a future in which Israel undergoes national repentance, is regathered to its land, experiences spiritual transformation, and becomes the center of a restored kingdom under the reign of Christ. These descriptions are detailed, geographic, and corporate in nature, and they have not yet been fulfilled in history. Because these prophecies remain outstanding, they cannot be reassigned or reinterpreted without altering their original meaning. Therefore, the future restoration of Israel stands as a necessary component of God's unfolding plan.

PART X — REVELATION AND THE RETURN TO ISRAEL

(A Structural Shift in Focus — Revelation 1–22)

Why This Section Matters

The book of Revelation provides the most detailed sequence of end-time events in scripture.

If:

- The Church has replaced Israel

Then we would expect:

The Church to remain the central focus throughout the book.

But if:

- God resumes His program with Israel

Then we should expect:

A shift in focus back to Israel.

The Divinely Given Outline of Revelation

Revelation 1:19

"Write the things which thou hast seen, and the things which are, and the things which shall be hereafter;"

Observations

This verse provides a three-part structure:

1. **Things which thou hast seen** → Chapter 1

2. **Things which are** → Chapters 2–3

3. **Things which shall be hereafter** → Chapters 4–22

Key phrase:

"Hereafter" — indicating a transition to a new phase

The Church in Chapters 2–3

Revelation 2–3

The Church is directly addressed:

"He that hath an ear, let him hear what the Spirit saith unto the churches."

Observations

- The Church is:
    o Named

    o Addressed

    o Corrected

    o Central

This is clearly the present age

The Transition to Chapter 4

Revelation 4:1

"After this I looked, and, behold, a door was opened in heaven… Come up hither, and I will shew thee things which must be hereafter."

Observations

- "After this" signals a structural shift
- The focus moves:
  - From earth → to heaven
  - From present → to future

This is not a continuation—it is a transition to coming events

---

The Absence of the Church After Chapter 3

From Chapter 4 onward:

- The Church is not addressed on earth
- The Church is not instructed on earth
- The Church is not described on earth
- The titles that Christ uses of Himself are no longer Church titles but are Jewish

This absence is:

- Immediate
- Complete
- Sustained

Key Question

If the Church has replaced Israel, why does it disappear from the narrative at this exact transition point?

The Appearance of the 24 Elders

Revelation 4:4

"And round about the throne were four and twenty seats: and upon the seats I saw four and twenty elders sitting, clothed in white raiment; and they had on their heads crowns of gold."

Observations

The elders are:

- Seated on thrones

- Clothed in white raiment

- Wearing crowns of gold

Compare with promises to the Church:

Revelation 3:21

"To him that overcometh will I grant to sit with me in my throne…"

Revelation 3:5

"He that overcometh… shall be clothed in white raiment…"

Revelation 2:10

"Be thou faithful unto death, and I will give thee **a crown of life**."

The Song of the 24 Elders

Revelation 5:9–10

"And they sung a new song, saying, Thou art worthy to take the book, and to open the seals thereof: for thou wast slain, and hast redeemed us to God by thy blood out of every kindred, and tongue, and people, and nation; And hast made us unto our God kings and priests: and we shall reign on the earth."

Observations from the Song

This passage adds critical clarity:

1. They are redeemed by the blood

"Thou… hast redeemed us to God by thy blood"

2. Their origin is global

"Out of every kindred, and tongue, and people, and nation"

3. Their identity is transformed

"Made us… kings and priests"

4. Their future includes reigning

"We shall reign on the earth"

The Significance of This Song

This is not:

- Angelic language

- Symbolic abstraction

It is:

The testimony of redeemed humanity now in heaven with their Lord

Important implications:

- They are **not Israel alone**

- They are drawn from **all nations**

- They are already:

    o Redeemed

    o Crowned

    o   Enthroned

Strong conclusion:

This group most naturally corresponds to:

The completed, glorified body of believers also known as the Church

Placement in the Timeline

This scene occurs:

- Before the seals are opened (Revelation 6)
- Before the tribulation judgments begin

Therefore:

This redeemed group is already:

In heaven prior to the unfolding of tribulation events

The Shift to a Jewish Framework

Beginning in Chapter 6, the focus changes dramatically back to the Jewish people and the Nation of Israel.

A. - The 144,000

Revelation 7:4–5

"And I heard the number of them which were sealed… Of the tribe of Juda were sealed twelve thousand…"

Observations:

- Tribes are named

- Identity is:

    o Ethnic

    o Specific

    o Jewish

This is unmistakably Israel

B. - The Temple and Jerusalem

Revelation 11:1–2

"Rise, and measure the temple of God… And the holy city shall they tread under foot…"

Observations:

- A temple is central

- A holy city is central

This is a Jewish framework

C. - The Woman in Revelation 12

Revelation 12:1–2, 5

"A woman clothed with the sun… And she brought forth a man child…"

Observations:

- The woman produces the Messiah

- The Messiah rules the nations

The woman represents:

Israel

The 70th Week Connection

Daniel 9:24

"Seventy weeks are determined upon thy people and upon thy holy city…"

- "Thy people" = Israel

- "Thy city" = Jerusalem

Revelation mirrors this with:

- 42 months

- 1260 days

Meaning:

Revelation resumes:

Israel's prophetic timeline

The Return of Christ to Israel

Revelation 19:11, 16

"Behold a white horse… KING OF KINGS, AND LORD OF LORDS."

Connected with:

Zechariah 14:4

"His feet shall stand… upon the mount of Olives…"

Observations:

- The return is:
  - Physical
  - Geographic
  - Located in Israel

The Full Convergence of This Section

When all elements are considered together:

1. The Church is central in Chapters 2–3

2. The Church is absent from the earthly narrative after Chapter

3. A redeemed group appears in heaven (24 elders)

4. That group sings of redemption from all nations

5. That group is crowned and enthroned before tribulation

6. The narrative shifts to:

- Israel
- Tribes
- Temple
- Jerusalem

7. Prophetic timelines tied to Israel resume

The Logical Conclusion

If:

- The Church is no longer the focus on earth

- A redeemed, completed group appears in heaven

- Israel-specific elements dominate the remainder

Then:

Revelation reflects a transition—not a replacement—returning the focus to Israel within the unfolding of end-time prophecy.

Final Thoughts on This Section

The structure of Revelation reveals a decisive shift in focus following the conclusion of the Church-centered messages in chapters 2 and 3. A redeemed and glorified group appears in heaven prior to the unfolding of tribulation events, identified by their song as those purchased from every nation and appointed to reign. From that point forward, the narrative is dominated by distinctly Israel-centered elements, including tribal identity, temple worship, Jerusalem as the focal point, and the continuation of prophetic timelines established in Daniel. This transition demonstrates not the replacement of Israel, but the resumption of God's dealings with Israel in fulfillment of previously established covenants and prophecies.

PART XI — THE TIMES OF THE GENTILES

(A Defined Period with a Defined End — Luke 21:24)

Why This Section Matters

Up to this point, we have established:

- The covenants remain in effect

- Israel's identity remains intact

- Israel's current condition is temporary

- Israel's future restoration is promised

Now we examine a statement made by Christ Himself that introduces a **time-bound framework** governing Israel's present condition:

The "Times of the Gentiles."

The Statement of Christ

Luke 21:24

"And they shall fall by the edge of the sword, and shall be led away captive into all nations: and Jerusalem shall be trodden down of the Gentiles, **until the times of the Gentiles be fulfilled.**"

Observations from the Text

This verse contains three distinct elements:

1. Judgment and scattering

"They shall… be led away captive into all nations"

2. Gentile domination

"Jerusalem shall be trodden down of the Gentiles"

3. A defined endpoint

"Until the times of the Gentiles be fulfilled"

The Significance of "Until"

The word **"until"** establishes a boundary.

It indicates:

- A beginning

- A duration

- An endpoint

Therefore:

This condition is:

Temporary, not permanent

What Are the "Times of the Gentiles"?

From the context, this phrase refers to a period in which:

- Jerusalem is under Gentile control

- Israel does not exercise full national authority

- Gentile influence dominates the land

This aligns with historical reality:

- Babylonian conquest

- Persian rule

- Greek control

- Roman occupation

- Continued foreign dominance

The Critical Implication

If the "Times of the Gentiles":

- Have a beginning
- Have a duration
- Have an endpoint

Then:

They must also come to an end

And when they end:

The condition they describe must also end.

What Ends When the Times Are Fulfilled?

The verse itself defines it:

"Jerusalem shall be trodden down of the Gentiles… until…"

Therefore:

When the "until" is reached:

- Jerusalem is no longer under Gentile domination
- Israel's status changes

This implies a restoration of Israel's authority and position

Connection to Israel's Present Condition

This statement explains something critical:

Why Israel is currently:

- Scattered (historically)
- Oppressed (historically)
- Not fully restored

Because they are within:

The Times of the Gentiles

Connection to Romans 11

Romans 11:25

"Blindness in part is happened to Israel, until the fullness of the Gentiles be come in."

Observations

Both passages include:

- Israel in a diminished condition

- Gentiles in a position of prominence

- A clearly defined **"until"**

These are not separate ideas.

They describe:

The same transitional period

The Logical Structure

When both passages are considered together:

- Israel is partially hardened

- Gentiles are in a period of prominence

- This condition continues **until a defined point**

- After that point, the condition changes

Israel's current condition is:

Time-bound and temporary

What This Means for Replacement Theology

Replacement theology requires:

- Israel's condition to be permanent

- Gentile inclusion to be final

- No return to Israel's prominence

But this passage teaches:

- Israel's condition has an endpoint

- Gentile dominance has an endpoint

Replacement cannot be permanent if the condition it depends on is temporary

---

The Broader Prophetic Alignment

This "until" structure aligns with:

- Deuteronomy 30 → restoration after scattering

- Romans 11 → future salvation of Israel

- Zechariah 12 → national repentance

- Revelation → return to Israel-focused events

Meaning:

This is not an isolated statement.

It fits within a **consistent prophetic framework**.

Final Thoughts on This Section

The statement of Christ in Luke 21:24 establishes a defined period in which Jerusalem is subject to Gentile domination, referred to as the "Times of the Gentiles." This period is explicitly described as temporary, marked by a clear beginning and a definitive endpoint. When considered alongside the parallel language in Romans 11, it becomes evident that Israel's present condition is not permanent but transitional. Because this period must come to an end, the conditions it describes—including Israel's diminished status—must also give way to a future restoration. Therefore, the concept of a permanent replacement of Israel is incompatible with the time-bound structure established by Christ Himself.

PART XII — THE EXPECTATION OF THE APOSTLES

(Post-Resurrection Understanding — Acts 1:6–7)

Why This Section Matters

At this point in the study, we have established:

- The covenants remain in effect

- Israel's identity remains intact

- Israel's current condition is temporary

- A future restoration is promised

Now we ask:

What did the apostles believe about Israel after the resurrection of Christ?

Why this is critical

If replacement theology were correct, we would expect:

- The apostles to understand that Israel's role had ended

- The kingdom promises to be redefined

- The focus to shift entirely away from national Israel

Instead, we examine what they actually ask.

The Question of the Apostles

Acts 1:6

"When they therefore were come together, they asked of him, saying, Lord, wilt thou at this time restore again the kingdom to Israel?"

Observations from the Question

This question reveals several key assumptions held by the apostles:

1. A Kingdom Will Be Restored

They expect:

A real, future kingdom of Israel would be restored as the prophets had promised.

2. The Kingdom Belongs to Israel

They do not ask:

- "Will you restore a spiritual kingdom?"

- "Will you give this to all nations equally?"

They ask:

"Restore again the kingdom to Israel"

3. The Restoration Is Future

They say:

"At this time…"

Summary

Their expectation includes:

- A **literal kingdom**

- A **national Israel focus**

- A **future fulfillment**

The Timing of This Question

This moment is crucial.

It occurs:

- After Christ's resurrection

- After 40 days of teaching

Acts 1:3

"To whom also he shewed himself alive after his passion… being seen of them forty days, and speaking of the things pertaining to the kingdom of God:"

Observations

- Jesus spent 40 days:

    o Teaching about the kingdom

- The apostles:

    o Still expect a restored kingdom to Israel

Critical implication

Their understanding was not:

- Corrected away from Israel

It remained:

Centered on Israel

The Response of Christ

Acts 1:7

"And he said unto them, It is not for you to know the times or the seasons, which the Father hath put in his own power."

Observations from the Response

Christ does **not** say:

- "You misunderstand the nature of the kingdom"
- "The kingdom is no longer for Israel"
- "Israel has been replaced"
- "The Church will inherit the blessings"

Instead, He addresses only:

The timing

This distinction is decisive

He corrects:

- When

He does not correct:

- What
- Who

What This Silence Means

In teaching, silence can be as important as speech.

If the apostles were wrong about:

- The kingdom being restored
- The kingdom belonging to Israel

Then this would be the moment to correct them.

But no correction is given

The Logical Conclusion

From this exchange:

- The expectation of a restored kingdom is valid

- The expectation that it belongs to Israel is valid

- The only unknown element is timing

Connection to Previous Sections

This aligns perfectly with:

- **Davidic Covenant** → a future throne in Israel

- **Romans 11** → future salvation of Israel and the Jews

- **Prophets** → national restoration in a completed sense

- **Revelation** → Israel-centered end-time events

Meaning

This is not an isolated expectation.

It is:

Consistent with the entire scriptural framework

Implication for Replacement Theology

Replacement theology requires that:

- Israel's kingdom promises are reinterpreted

- The apostles misunderstood the teachings of Christ

- The kingdom is no longer tied to Israel but shared among the nations

But this passage shows:

- The apostles held a literal expectation

- Christ did not correct that expectation

Therefore:

The expectation of a restored kingdom to Israel stands

Final Thoughts for This Section

The question posed by the apostles in Acts 1:6 demonstrates that, even after the resurrection and extensive instruction from Christ concerning the kingdom of God, they continued to expect a literal restoration of the kingdom to Israel and its people. Christ's response does not correct this expectation but instead redirects their focus away from the timing of its fulfillment. This distinction is critical, as it confirms that the concept of a restored kingdom for Israel remained valid within apostolic understanding. Therefore, the idea that Israel's role in scripture had been replaced or redefined is not supported by this passage, but rather stands in direct tension with it.

PART XIII — THE CONSISTENCY OF LITERAL FULFILLMENT

Why This Section Matters

Many of the disagreements surrounding Israel and the Church do not come from:

- Different verses

- Different manuscripts

They come from:

Different methods of interpretation

Specifically:

- First-coming prophecies are taken **literally**

- Second-coming and kingdom prophecies are often taken **symbolically**

This section asks a simple but critical question:

Does scripture itself justify that shift—or does it demonstrate consistency?

The Principle to Be Tested

The principle under examination is:

Prophecies that are specific and measurable are fulfilled literally unless the text clearly indicates otherwise.

We now test this principle against fulfilled prophecy.

The Birthplace of the Messiah

Micah 5:2

"But thou, Bethlehem Ephratah… out of thee shall he come forth unto me that is to be ruler in Israel…"

Fulfillment:

Matthew 2:1

"Now when Jesus was born in Bethlehem of Judaea…"

Observation

- Prophecy specified:
    - A precise location
- Fulfillment occurred:
    - In that exact location

No symbolic reinterpretation was applied

The Lineage of the Messiah

2 Samuel 7:12

"I will set up thy seed after thee…"

Fulfillment:

Luke 3:31

(Tracing lineage back to David)

Observation

- The prophecy required:
    - A literal descendant

- The fulfillment confirms:
  - A literal lineage

Again:

No redefinition occurred.

The Manner of Death

Psalm 22:16

"They pierced my hands and my feet…"

Fulfillment:

John 20:25

"Except I shall see in his hands the print of the nails…"

Observation

- The prophecy described:
  - A specific form of death
- The fulfillment matched:
  - That exact description

No symbolic reinterpretation

The Burial of the Messiah

Isaiah 53:9

"He made his grave with the wicked, and with the rich in his death…"

Fulfillment:

Matthew 27:57–60

"A rich man… Joseph… laid it in his own new tomb…"

Observation

- Even secondary details:
    - Wealth of the burial provider
- Were fulfilled:
    - Literally

The Pattern Established

From these examples:

- Location → literal
- Lineage → literal
- Death → literal
- Burial → literal

Pattern:

Specific prophecy → literal fulfillment

Applying the Same Standard Forward

Now we return to Israel-related prophecies:

Land boundaries (Genesis 15)

National restoration (Ezekiel 36–37)

Throne of David (2 Samuel 7)

Kingdom centered in Jerusalem (Isaiah 2)

These are:

- Specific

- Geographic

- Measurable

Therefore:

They meet the same criteria as first-coming prophecies.

The Inconsistency Problem

If someone claims:

- First-coming prophecies → literal

- Israel/kingdom prophecies → symbolic

Then they must answer:

Why does the method change?

This creates a contradiction:

The same type of language is:

- Literal in one case

- Symbolic in another

The Absence of Scriptural Justification

Now we ask:

Where does scripture instruct us to reinterpret these later promises symbolically instead of literally like all the previous prophecies?

The answer:

It does not.

Therefore:

The shift in interpretation is:

- Imposed externally
- Not derived from the text itself

The Logical Conclusion

If:

- God fulfilled detailed prophecies literally in the past
- The future promises are equally detailed
- No reinterpretation is given

Then:

Future prophecies must be expected to be fulfilled literally as well

---

Implication for Israel

This directly affects:

- The land promise
- The kingdom promise
- The restoration promise

Meaning:

These cannot be:

- Abstracted

- Reassigned

- Spiritualized away

Final Thoughts for This Section

The consistent pattern of fulfilled prophecy in scripture demonstrates that specific and measurable predictions are realized in a literal and precise manner. This pattern is evident in the prophecies surrounding the first coming of Christ, where details concerning location, lineage, death, and burial were fulfilled exactly as stated. Because future prophecies concerning Israel, the kingdom, and the reign of Christ are presented with the same level of specificity, there is no textual basis for applying a different interpretive method to them. Therefore, the expectation of a literal fulfillment remains the most consistent and textually supported approach, and any departure from this standard introduces inconsistency into the interpretation of scripture.

PART XIV — THE PROPHETIC PATTERN OF ISRAEL'S FEASTS

(God's Appointed Times as a Prophetic Timeline — Leviticus 23)

Why This Section Matters

Up to this point, we have examined:

- Covenants

- Identity

- Prophecy

- Structure

Now we examine something different:

A recurring, cyclical system established by God Himself

The key idea:

The feasts of Israel are not merely:

- Ceremonial

- Cultural

- Historical

They are:

Prophetic appointments ("moedim") built into time

The Establishment of the Feasts

Leviticus 23:1–2

"And the Lord spake unto Moses, saying, Speak unto the children of Israel, and say unto them, Concerning the feasts of the Lord… even these are my feasts."

Observations

- These are not:
  - Israel's inventions

They are:

"The feasts of the Lord"

Meaning:

They originate from:

God's design, not human tradition

The Structure of the Feasts

There are seven primary feasts:

Spring Feasts (First Group)

1. Passover
2. Unleavened Bread
3. Firstfruits
4. Pentecost

Fall Feasts (Second Group)

5. Trumpets
6. Day of Atonement

7. Tabernacles

The Spring Feasts and Their Fulfillment

Passover

Leviticus 23:5

"In the fourteenth day… is the Lord's passover."

Fulfillment:

Christ's crucifixion as the sacrificial lamb

Unleavened Bread

Leviticus 23:6

"Seven days ye must eat unleavened bread."

Fulfillment:

- Sinless nature of Christ

- Burial (absence of corruption)

Firstfruits

Leviticus 23:10–11

"Ye shall bring a sheaf of the firstfruits…"

Fulfillment:

- Resurrection of Jesus Christ

Pentecost

Leviticus 23:15–16

"Count unto you… fifty days…"

Fulfillment:

- Outpouring of the Spirit
- Beginning of the Church (Acts 2)

Observations on the Spring Feasts

All four spring feasts were:

- Fulfilled
- Precisely
- In order
- Historically

This establishes a pattern:

God fulfills His appointed times exactly as scheduled

The Gap Between the Feasts

Between Pentecost and Trumpets:

- There is a **gap of time**
- No major feast occurs

This corresponds to:

- The current age
- The period of Gentile inclusion

Important:

This gap was:

Built into the calendar from the beginning

The Fall Feasts — Not Yet Fulfilled

Trumpets

Leviticus 23:24

"A memorial of blowing of trumpets…"

Day of Atonement

Leviticus 23:27

"A day of atonement…"

Tabernacles

Leviticus 23:34

"The feast of tabernacles…"

Observations

These feasts:

- Have not yet been fulfilled in the same precise way
- Are connected to:
  - Repentance
  - Judgment

o Dwelling with God

These align with:

- Israel's future repentance

- Christ's return

- The kingdom age

The Prophetic Implication

If:

- Spring feasts were fulfilled literally

- Fall feasts remain unfulfilled

Then:

The prophetic calendar is incomplete

Connection to Israel

These feasts were given to:

Israel as a nation

Therefore:

Their fulfillment must involve:

- The same group

- The same framework

This reinforces:

Israel's ongoing role in prophecy

The Consistency with Previous Sections

This aligns with:

- Covenants → not fully fulfilled

- Romans 11 → future restoration

- Prophets → national repentance

- Revelation → future events

The Logical Conclusion

If:

- God fulfilled the first set of feasts precisely

- The second set remains unfulfilled

- The pattern is consistent

Then:

The remaining feasts must also be fulfilled in the future

Final Thoughts for This Section

The feasts of Israel, established by God in Leviticus 23, function not only as ceremonial observances but as prophetic appointments embedded within the structure of time. The precise and literal fulfillment of the spring feasts in connection with the first coming of Christ establishes a clear pattern of fulfillment. The fall feasts, which remain unfulfilled in the same manner, point forward to future events involving repentance, restoration, and the establishment of God's kingdom. Because these appointed times were given specifically to Israel and have been only partially fulfilled, they provide further evidence that God's prophetic program concerning Israel is ongoing and not yet complete.

PART XV — ISRAEL'S FUTURE ROLE AMONG THE NATIONS

(Central Position in the Kingdom — Zechariah 8:23)

Why This Section Matters

Many interpretations allow for:

- A general future kingdom

But remove:

- Israel's central role within it

This section tests that idea directly:

Does scripture describe Israel as central—or absorbed into something larger?

The Direct Statement of Zechariah

Zechariah 8:23

"Thus saith the Lord of hosts; In those days it shall come to pass, that ten men shall take hold out of all languages of the nations… shall take hold of the skirt of him that is a Jew, saying, We will go with you: for we have heard that God is with you."

Observations from the Text

This verse contains several critical elements:

1. A future time frame

"In those days…"

2. Global participation

"Out of all languages of the nations"

3. A specific identity

"Him that is a Jew"

4. A directional movement

"We will go with you"

5. A spiritual recognition

"God is with you"

The Relationship Defined

The nations are:

- Seeking God

- Recognizing His presence

But how?

Through Israel

This establishes a structure:

- Nations → seeking

- Israel → central

- God → dwelling among them

What This Passage Does NOT Say

It does not say:

- "We will go directly without distinction"

- "Israel is no longer relevant"

- "All identities are dissolved"

Instead, it maintains:

A clear distinction and role

Supporting Prophecy — Nations Flow to Jerusalem

Isaiah 2:2–3

"All nations shall flow unto it… For out of Zion shall go forth the law, and the word of the Lord from Jerusalem."

Observations

- Location:

    o Jerusalem

- Authority:

    o The Lord

- Movement:

    o Nations coming to Israel

This reinforces:

Israel as:

The center of divine governance

Israel as a Blessing to the Nations

This fulfills the original promise:

Genesis 12:3

"In thee shall all families of the earth be blessed."

Observation

This promise is:

- Not canceled

- Not redefined

It is:

Realized through Israel's restored position

The Reign of Christ from Israel

Zechariah 14:9

"And the Lord shall be king over all the earth…"

Combined with:

- Jerusalem as the center

- Israel as the host nation

Result:

A global kingdom with:

Israel at its center and Christ as its head

The Role of the Nations

The nations are not:

- Eliminated

- Absorbed

They are:

- Present

- Active

- Submitting to divine rule

But their relationship is:

Oriented toward Israel

The Logical Structure

From all these passages:

- Christ reigns

- From Jerusalem

- Over all nations

- With Israel as the central nation

The Implication for Replacement Theology

Replacement theology requires:

- Israel to lose distinction

- Israel to lose centrality

- Israel to lose identity

But these passages show:

- Israel is distinct

- Israel is central

- Israel is recognized by the nations

The Logical Conclusion

If:

- Nations seek God through Israel

- Christ reigns from Israel

- Jerusalem is the center

Then:

Israel cannot be replaced—it is essential to the structure of the kingdom

---

Final Thoughts for This Section

The prophetic scriptures consistently describe a future in which Israel occupies a central and distinct role among the nations under the reign of Christ. The nations are depicted not as replacing Israel, but as coming to it, recognizing God's presence among His people and seeking His guidance through them. Jerusalem serves as the focal point of divine governance, and Israel functions as the channel through which the blessings of God extend to the world. Because this structure preserves Israel's identity and elevates its role within the kingdom, it stands in direct opposition to the concept of replacement, confirming instead that Israel remains an essential component of God's unfolding plan.

PART XVI — HISTORICAL CONFIRMATION OF THE SCRIPTURAL PATTERN

Purpose of This Section

This section does not establish doctrine.

Scripture has already done that.

Instead, this section asks:

Does history align with the pattern already revealed in scripture?

Important boundary

We are not arguing:

- History defines scripture

We are examining:

Whether history reflects what scripture predicted

The Predicted Global Scattering

Deuteronomy 28:64

"And the Lord shall scatter thee among all people, from the one end of the earth even unto the other…"

Observations

- The scattering is:
    - Global
    - Extensive

  o Long-term

Historical Alignment

The Jewish people were:

- Dispersed across continents

- Found in:

  o Europe

  o Africa

  o Asia

  o The Middle East

This matches the description:

"From one end of the earth even unto the other"

The Preservation of Israel

Jeremiah 30:11

"Though I make a full end of all nations whither I have scattered thee, yet will I not make a full end of thee…"

Observations

- Israel is:

  o Judged

  o Scattered

But: not destroyed

Historical Reality

Despite:

- Repeated persecution

- Attempts at elimination

- Loss of land and sovereignty

Israel:

- Maintained identity

- Retained cultural continuity

- Remained a distinct people

The Predicted Regathering

Deuteronomy 30:3–4

"The Lord thy God will... gather thee from all the nations..."

Ezekiel 36:24

"I will take you from among the heathen, and gather you out of all countries, and will bring you into your own land."

Observations

- The regathering is:

    o Global

    o Directed

    o Land-specific

The Modern Reestablishment of Israel

In 1948:

- The State of Israel was established

- A dispersed people returned

- National identity was restored

Observations

This event reflects:

- Regathering

- Re-identification as a nation

- Return to a defined geographic land

Necessary Clarification

This event does **not** fulfill all prophecy.

It does not include:

- National repentance

- Full spiritual transformation

- The reign of Jesus Christ

Therefore:

It is not: **the completion**

But it is:

A continuation of the process described in scripture

The Uniqueness of This Historical Pattern

No other nation in recorded history has:

- Been scattered globally

- Maintained identity for centuries

- Returned to its original land

- Re-established national sovereignty

This makes Israel:

Historically unique

Alignment with the Scriptural Sequence

Compare the pattern:

Scripture describes:

1. Scattering

2. Preservation

3. Regathering

4. Restoration

History shows:

1. Scattering (has happened)

2. Preservation (has happened)

3. Regathering (partial)

4. Full restoration (not yet)

The Logical Conclusion

If:

- Scripture predicts a sequence

- History reflects that sequence

- The sequence is not yet complete

Then:

The process is ongoing

The Implication for Israel's Future

This means:

- Israel's existence today is not accidental

- Israel's presence in the land is not irrelevant

- Israel's identity remains intact

Therefore:

Israel must still be:

Part of an unfolding prophetic framework

The Implication for Replacement Theology

Replacement theology assumes:

- Israel's role has ended in the national sense

- The promises are fulfilled or reassigned

But history shows:

- Israel still exists

- Israel has returned

- Israel remains distinct

Therefore:

The assumption of replacement does not match observable reality

---

Final Thoughts for This Section

The historical record reflects a pattern that closely parallels the sequence described in scripture concerning Israel. The global scattering of the Jewish people, their preservation as a distinct identity over extended periods including their native language, and their partial regathering to the land all align with the prophetic framework established in the covenants and writings of the prophets. While the full spiritual and national restoration of Israel remains future, the developments observed in history demonstrate that the process described in scripture is ongoing rather than complete. This alignment provides an additional layer of confirmation that the promises concerning Israel remain active and are continuing toward their ultimate fulfillment in God's ultimate plan.

PART XVII — GOD'S OATH AND UNCONDITIONAL PROMISES

Why This Section Is Foundational

Up to this point, we have established that:

- God made promises to Abraham

- Those promises are described as everlasting

- Those promises have not yet been fully fulfilled

Now we move deeper:

What guarantees that those promises cannot be altered, revoked, or reassigned?

The answer is not simply:

- That God spoke

But that:

God swore an oath

The Oath Declared by God

Genesis 22:16–18

"By myself have I sworn, saith the Lord, for because thou hast done this thing… That in blessing I will bless thee, and in multiplying I will multiply thy seed… And in thy seed shall all the nations of the earth be blessed…"

Observations from the Text

This passage introduces something unique:

1. God swears an oath

"By myself have I sworn"

2. The oath is self-referential

- God does not swear by:
    - Creation
    - Law
    - Another authority

He swears by:

Himself

The Significance of Swearing "By Myself"

This is one of the strongest forms of commitment found in scripture.

Why?

Because:

- There is no authority higher than God
- There is nothing greater to guarantee the promise
- God's own character is on the line

Therefore:

The promise is anchored in:

God's own nature and character

The New Testament Confirmation

Hebrews 6:13–18

"For when God made promise to Abraham, because he could swear by no greater, he sware by himself… That by two immutable things, in which it was impossible for God to lie…"

Observations

This passage explains the earlier oath:

1. God could swear by no greater

→ Therefore He swore by Himself

2. Two immutable things

- The promise
- The oath

3. Impossible for God to lie

Meaning:

The promise is not only declared—

It is legally and morally secured by God's own nature

The Relationship to the Law

A common argument is:

"Israel broke the Law—therefore the promises are forfeited"

Scripture directly addresses this:

Galatians 3:17

"The covenant, that was confirmed before of God in Christ, the law… cannot disannul, that it should make the promise of none effect."

Observations

- The Law came:
  - **After** the promise
- The Law:
  - Does not cancel the promise

Therefore:

Israel's failure under the Law:

Cannot nullify the Abrahamic covenant

The Logical Structure of This Argument

Putting these passages together:

1. God made a promise to Abraham

2. God confirmed that promise with an oath

3. The oath is grounded in God Himself

4. The Law does not cancel that promise

5. God cannot lie or change

Therefore:

The promise cannot be revoked, reassigned, or redefined

The Implication for Replacement Theology

Replacement theology requires that:

- The promises to Abraham:
    - Be transferred
    - Or reinterpreted

But this creates a direct conflict:

If God swore:

"By myself…"

Then altering that promise would mean:

- The oath did not hold
- The guarantee failed

Which leads to an unavoidable conclusion:

To cancel or transfer the promise is to undermine the oath itself

---

The Deeper Theological Issue

This is no longer just about Israel.

It becomes:

A question of whether God binds Himself to His own word

If He does:

- The covenant stands

If He does not:

- No promise is secure

Final Thoughts for This Section

The promises made to Abraham were not merely spoken but were confirmed by a divine oath in which God swore by Himself, grounding the covenant in His own unchanging nature and name. The New Testament affirms that this oath, together with the original promise, constitutes an immutable foundation that cannot be annulled, even by the later introduction of the Law or by human disobedience. Because it is impossible for God to lie or to violate His own nature, the covenant remains binding and unalterable. Therefore, any interpretation that reassigns or nullifies these promises stands in direct tension with the oath by which they were secured, and the fulfillment of those promises must still take place as originally given.

PART XVIII — ISRAEL'S UNIQUE STATUS AMONG THE NATIONS

Why This Section Matters

Up to this point, we have demonstrated:

- God made unconditional promises

- Those promises are secured by His oath

- Those promises are secured by His character

- Those promises cannot be annulled

Now we ask:

Who are those promises tied to—and can that identity be reassigned?

This section answers by showing:

Scripture consistently treats Israel as a nation with a unique and permanent status among all nations

The "Full End" Distinction

Jeremiah 46:28

"Fear thou not, O Jacob my servant, saith the Lord: for I am with thee; for I will make a full end of all the nations whither I have driven thee: **but I will not make a full end of thee**, but correct thee in measure…"

Observations from the Text

This verse establishes a direct comparison:

1. Other nations

"I will make a full end of all the nations…"

2. Israel

"But I will not make a full end of thee"

The Significance of This Distinction

This is not a general statement.

It is:

- Absolute
- Comparative
- Intentional

Meaning:

Israel is placed in a category that is:

Different from all other nations

The Nature of That Difference

Other nations:

- Rise
- Fall
- Disappear

Israel:

- Is judged

- Is scattered

- But is never eliminated

This establishes:

Perpetual national continuity

The Permanence of Israel as a Nation

Jeremiah 31:35–36

"Thus saith the Lord, which giveth the sun for a light by day… If those ordinances depart from before me… then the seed of Israel also shall cease from being a nation before me for ever."

Observations

Israel's existence is tied to:

- The sun

- The moon

- The fixed order of creation

This is not symbolic language

It is:

A measurable, observable standard

The Strength of This Comparison

The condition is stated as:

If creation collapses → Israel ceases

Therefore:

As long as:

- The sun rises

- The moon remains

Israel remains a nation before God

The Identity of Israel Is Maintained Even in Judgment

Amos 9:9

"I will sift the house of Israel among all nations… yet shall not the least grain fall upon the earth."

Observations

- Israel is:

    o Scattered

    o Sifted

    o Tested

But:

Not lost or done away with

Meaning:

Even dispersion does not erase identity.

Israel Distinguished from All Peoples

Deuteronomy 7:6

"For thou art an holy people unto the Lord thy God: the Lord thy God hath chosen thee to be a special people unto himself, above all people that are upon the face of the earth."

Observations

Israel is described as:

- Chosen

- Set apart

- Above all peoples

Important:

This is not:

- Temporary language

- Conditional language

It defines:

Identity and role

The Logical Structure of This Section

When these passages are combined:

1. Israel will not come to a full end

2. Israel's existence is tied to creation

3. Israel is preserved through scattering

4. Israel is chosen and set apart

Therefore:

Israel is uniquely and permanently distinct among all nations of the world

---

The Implication for Replacement Theology

Replacement theology requires:

- Israel's identity to be:
    - Absorbed
    - Reassigned
    - Reinterpreted

But this creates a contradiction:

If Israel is:

- Never brought to an end
- Permanently defined as a nation

Then:

Its identity cannot be transferred to another group

The Core Conclusion

This is not simply about:

- Survival

It is about:

A divinely preserved national identity with a specific role given by the creator of the universe

Final Thoughts for This Section

Scripture consistently presents Israel as a nation possessing a unique and enduring status among all the peoples of the earth. Unlike other nations, which may rise and fall or even come to a full end, Israel is explicitly declared to be preserved, corrected, and sustained without being destroyed. Its continued existence is tied to the stability of the created order itself, establishing a permanence that transcends historical circumstances. Because this identity is defined and preserved by God, it cannot be reassigned or absorbed into another entity without contradicting the explicit statements of scripture. Therefore, Israel remains a distinct and enduring nation within the framework of God's plan.

PART XIX — GOD'S FAITHFULNESS AND UNCHANGING CHARACTER

Why This Section Matters

All previous sections ultimately depend on one foundational truth:

God's character determines the reliability of His promises

If God is:

- Consistent

- Faithful

- Unchanging

Then:

His covenants must remain exactly as declared

But if His character is flexible:

- Promises could shift

- Meaning could change

Therefore:

This section addresses the core issue:

Does God remain consistent with His own word?

The Direct Statement of God's Nature

Malachi 3:6

"For I am the Lord, I change not; therefore ye sons of Jacob are not consumed."

Observations from the Text

This verse contains two connected truths:

1. God does not change

"I change not"

2. Israel continues because of this

"Therefore ye sons of Jacob are not consumed"

The Logical Connection

The verse does not present these ideas separately.

It directly links them together:

Because God does not change → Israel is not destroyed

Meaning:

Israel's continued existence is:

A direct result of God's unchanging nature

God's Truthfulness

Numbers 23:19

"God is not a man, that he should lie; neither the son of man, that he should repent: hath he said, and shall he not do it? or hath he spoken, and shall he not make it good?"

Observations

God is described as:

- Not a liar

- Not one who changes intention

- One who fulfills what He speaks

The Structure of the Statement

The verse presents a sequence:

1. God speaks

2. God does

3. God fulfills

There is no category for:

- Retraction

- Reinterpretation

- Reassignment

The Reliability of God's Word

Isaiah 55:11

"So shall my word be that goeth forth out of my mouth: it shall not return unto me void..."

Observations

God's word:

- Goes forth with purpose

- Accomplishes what He intends

- Does not fail

The Implication for Covenant Promises

If:

- God does not change

- God does not lie

- God's word does not fail

Then:

His covenant declarations must remain fixed

The Problem Introduced by Reinterpretation

Replacement theology requires:

- Changing the meaning of promises

- Reassigning recipients

- Spiritualizing concrete language

This introduces a conflict:

If the meaning changes:

- The original statement is no longer intact

Which implies:

God's words did not mean what they originally said

The Broader Theological Impact

This issue extends beyond Israel.

If God's promises can be reinterpreted:

- Salvation promises could be redefined

- Eternal life could be reinterpreted

- Assurance could become uncertain

Therefore:

The issue is not limited to one doctrine—

It affects the entire structure of faith

The Consistency of God Across Scripture

From Genesis to Revelation:

- God speaks

- God declares

- God fulfills

There is no pattern where:

- God permanently reverses unconditional promises

Therefore:

To introduce such a reversal:

Breaks the established pattern of scripture

The Logical Conclusion

If:

- God is unchanging

- God cannot lie

- God fulfills His word

Then:

His promises must remain as originally given

Final Thoughts for This Section

The unchanging nature of God serves as the ultimate foundation for the reliability of His promises. Scripture consistently affirms that God does not alter His character, does not speak falsely, and does not fail to accomplish what He has declared. The continued preservation of Israel is explicitly tied to this unchanging nature, demonstrating that God's covenantal commitments remain in effect despite human failure. Any interpretation that redefines or reassigns these promises introduces a contradiction between God's stated character and the meaning of His words. Therefore, the enduring validity of the promises made to Israel is not merely a matter of interpretation, but a direct reflection of the faithfulness and consistency of God Himself.

PART XX — THE DANGERS OF REPLACEMENT THEOLOGY

Why This Section Matters

The purpose of this study has not been:

- To win an argument

- To elevate one system over another

It has been:

To determine whether scripture can be allowed to speak as written

Now we examine the consequences of rejecting that approach.

Important clarification

This section is not:

- A judgment of individuals

- A statement about motives

It is an evaluation of:

The theological implications of a system of interpretation

The Stability of God's Promises

Replacement theology requires that:

- Promises made to Israel

- Are either:

  o Reassigned

- o   Redefined

- o   Or fulfilled in a different way than originally stated

This introduces a critical question:

When God makes a promise, is its meaning fixed?

Numbers 23:19

"Hath he said, and shall he not do it? or hath he spoken, and shall he not make it good?"

Observations

- God's words are:

  - o   Directly tied to action

- What He says:

  - o   He performs

Implication

If the meaning of a promise can change:

The connection between what God said and what God does is weakened considerably. Allowing for this type of understanding also must allow for God to change what he does on almost any other theological doctrine in scripture. Can God simply change His meaning of what is acceptable to him for salvation? Only the blood of Jesus Christ is sufficient for the forgiveness of sins according to scripture. Can we also say that he has changed his meaning of what is acceptable? The answer is, absolutely not.

The Meaning of Covenant Language

Throughout scripture, God uses terms such as:

- "Everlasting"

- "Forever"

- "Perpetual"

Genesis 17:7

"I will establish my covenant… for an everlasting covenant…"

Observations

These terms are:

- Clear

- Repeated

- Foundational to covenant language

Replacement theology requires these to be:

- Reinterpreted

- Contextually altered

Implication

If "everlasting" does not mean:

- Everlasting

Then:

Language loses fixed meaning

The Introduction of Interpretive Subjectivity

Replacement theology depends on:

- Reading beyond the plain meaning

- Assigning symbolic fulfillment to literal statements

- Reassigning recipients of promises

This creates a shift:

From:

- Text-driven interpretation

To:

- System-driven interpretation

Result

Meaning becomes:

Dependent on the interpreter rather than the text

The Breakdown of Prophetic Structure

If Israel is removed from its role:

- Land promises lose geographic meaning

- The kingdom loses national structure

- Prophetic timelines lose continuity

- God's Word looses clarity

What remains is:

- Generalized fulfillment

- Abstract interpretation

Implication

Prophecy becomes:

Detached from measurable reality

The Warning Given to Gentiles

Romans 11:18

"Boast not against the branches…"

Observations

Gentiles are warned:

- Not to assume superiority
- Not to assume permanence
- Not to disregard Israel's place

Replacement theology asserts:

- A permanent shift
- A completed transfer

Therefore:

It moves in the direction that scripture explicitly warns against

---

The Impact on Assurance

Believers rely on:

- The certainty of God's promises
- The reliability of His word

If one set of promises can be reinterpreted:

Then logically:

- Any promise could be reinterpreted

This affects:

- Assurance of salvation

- Confidence in prophecy

- Trust in God's word

The Broader Theological Consequence

This issue extends beyond Israel.

It affects:

- The nature of covenant

- The stability of language

- The method of interpretation

- The character of God

The Core Issue Restated

At its deepest level, the question is:

Does God mean what He says?

If yes:

- The promises to Israel stand

If no:

- All promises become uncertain

The Logical Chain of Consequences

If replacement theology is accepted:

1. Promises can be reassigned

2. Language becomes flexible

3. Interpretation becomes subjective

4. Prophecy becomes abstract

5. Assurance becomes weakened

The Final Logical Conclusion

Because:

- Scripture presents God as unchanging

- Scripture presents His word as reliable

- Scripture presents His covenants as enduring

Then:

Any system requiring reinterpretation of those elements introduces instability into the entire framework of scripture

---

Final Thoughts for This Section

The acceptance of replacement theology introduces significant theological instability by requiring the reinterpretation of clear covenantal language and the reassignment of promises originally given to Israel. This approach weakens the connection between God's declarations and their fulfillment, alters the meaning of foundational terms such as "everlasting," and shifts interpretation away from the text toward the framework of the interpreter. As a result, the reliability of prophetic structure is diminished, and the assurance derived from

God's promises is placed on uncertain ground. Therefore, the issue extends beyond the identity of Israel and the Church and reaches into the fundamental question of whether God's words retain their original meaning and whether His promises remain fixed and trustworthy.

PART XXI — FULL REBUTTALS

Rebuttal 1 — "The Church Is the New Israel"

The claim that the Church has replaced Israel is one of the central assertions of replacement theology. It proposes that the identity, promises, and role of Israel have been transferred to the Church, such that the Church now functions as the "true Israel" in the plan of God.

For this claim to be valid, it must be demonstrated from scripture that one of the following has occurred:

1. Israel has been permanently rejected by God

2. Israel's identity has been redefined

3. Israel's promises have been reassigned to another entity

If none of these can be clearly established from the text, then the claim cannot stand.

We begin by examining whether scripture teaches that Israel has been rejected.

Romans 11:1

"I say then, Hath God cast away his people? God forbid…"

This passage is decisive in its clarity. The question being asked is not implied—it is explicit:

Has God rejected Israel?

The answer given is equally explicit:

"God forbid."

This phrase represents the strongest possible denial in the language of the New Testament. It is not a qualified answer. It is not conditional. It is absolute.

The verse continues:

"For I also am an Israelite…"

Paul's appeal here is significant. He does not argue abstractly. He appeals to identity. He himself is an Israelite, and yet he is not cast away. This demonstrates that Israel, as a category, is still recognized and still valid within the framework of God's ultimate plan.

The argument is extended further:

Romans 11:2

"God hath not cast away his people which he foreknew."

This introduces a second layer:

- Israel is not only not rejected

- Israel is still "His people"

The phrase "which he foreknew" connects Israel's identity to God's prior covenantal relationship. It is not being redefined—it is being reaffirmed.

The passage then moves forward in time:

Romans 11:25

"Blindness in part is happened to Israel, until the fullness of the Gentiles be come in."

This verse is critical for understanding Israel's present condition.

Israel is described as:

- Partially blinded

- Temporarily affected

- Existing within a defined period ("until")

The presence of the word "until" is decisive.

It indicates:

- A beginning

- A duration

- An endpoint

This means Israel's current condition is not permanent.

It is transitional and for a purpose

The passage concludes with a future statement:

Romans 11:26

"And so all Israel shall be saved…"

This statement cannot be ignored or redefined without altering the plain meaning of the text.

Israel is:

- Still called Israel

- Still expected to exist in the future

- Still the subject of a coming salvation

At this point, the logical structure becomes clear:

If Israel were replaced by the Church:

- Israel would no longer exist as a meaningful category

- Israel would not be described as having a future

- Israel would not be the subject of future salvation

But scripture presents the opposite:

- Israel exists

- Israel is distinct

- Israel has a future

At no point in this passage is there:

- A redefinition of Israel

- A transfer of identity

- A merging of Israel into the Church

Instead, what we see is:

- Continuity of identity

- Temporary alteration of condition

- Future restoration

The claim that the Church is the new Israel requires a step that the text never takes.

It requires moving from:

"Gentiles are included in blessing"

to:

"Israel is no longer Israel"

That step is not found in scripture.

Final Thoughts on Rebuttal 1

The argument that the Church replaces Israel cannot be sustained when the full testimony of scripture is considered. Israel is explicitly stated to be un-rejected, continues to be identified as a distinct people, and is described as having a future restoration. The Church participates in the blessings of God but is never defined as replacing Israel. Therefore, the concept of replacement is not supported by the text, but instead stands in direct tension with it.

Rebuttal 2 — "The Promises Are Fulfilled Spiritually"

A second major argument presented in support of replacement theology is that the promises given to Israel—particularly those involving land, kingdom, and national identity—are not to be understood in a literal or physical sense, but are instead fulfilled spiritually in the Church.

This view does not always deny the promises themselves. Rather, it redefines their nature and understanding. What was originally expressed in concrete, measurable terms is interpreted as symbolic language pointing to spiritual realities.

To evaluate this claim, we must ask a foundational question:

Does scripture itself indicate that these promises should be reinterpreted symbolically, or does it present them as literal commitments intended to be fulfilled as originally stated?

The Nature of the Original Promises

We begin with the covenantal promises themselves.

Genesis 15:18

"Unto thy seed have I given this land, from the river of Egypt unto the great river, the river Euphrates:"

This statement is not abstract.

It defines:

- A specific people ("thy seed")

- A specific possession ("this land")

- Specific boundaries ("from… unto…")

Observations

This language is:

- Geographic

- Measurable

- Bounded

It does not describe:

- A general spiritual condition

- A symbolic inheritance

- A non-physical reality

Therefore:

The promise, as given, is:

Concrete in nature and definable in real-world terms

The Pattern of Fulfillment in Scripture

To understand how such promises should be interpreted, we must examine how God has fulfilled prophecy in the past.

Example: The Birth of the Messiah

Micah 5:2

"But thou, Bethlehem Ephratah… out of thee shall he come forth…"

Fulfillment:

Matthew 2:1

"Jesus was born in Bethlehem…"

Observation

- A specific location was predicted
- That exact location was fulfilled

Example: The Death of the Messiah

Psalm 22:16

"They pierced my hands and my feet…"

Fulfillment:

John 20:25

"The print of the nails…"

Observation

- A specific manner of death was described
- That exact manner occurred

Pattern Established

From these and many other examples:

- Specific prophecy → literal fulfillment
- Measurable detail → exact realization

This establishes a consistent interpretive principle:

When God speaks in specific, concrete terms, those terms are fulfilled as given

Applying This Pattern to Israel's Promises

Now we return to the promises given to Israel:

- Land → defined boundaries

- Kingdom → throne and rule

- Nation → identifiable people

These promises are:

- As specific as the prophecies of Christ's first coming

- Equally measurable

- Equally concrete

Therefore the question becomes:

Why would these promises suddenly shift from literal to symbolic?

The Inconsistency Problem

If we interpret:

- Bethlehem → literal

- Crucifixion → literal

But then interpret:

- Land → symbolic

- Kingdom → spiritual only

Then we are applying:

Two different interpretive systems to the same type of language

This creates inconsistency.

The Absence of Scriptural Redefinition

For the "spiritual fulfillment" argument to hold, scripture would need to explicitly redefine the terms clearly. We should also see the apostles clearly teaching these newly revealed truths.

We would expect statements such as:

- "The land promise now refers to a spiritual inheritance"

- "Israel now represents the Church"

- "Jerusalem now represents a non-geographic reality"

But no such statements are given.

Instead:

- Israel continues to be called Israel

- Jerusalem continues to be treated as a real place

- The land continues to be described geographically

The Logical Consequence of Spiritualization

If the original meaning of the promise is altered:

- The promise is no longer being fulfilled as given

- It is being reinterpreted after the fact

This introduces a critical issue:

The meaning of the promise is no longer controlled by the text, but by the interpreter

Connection to the Character of God

Earlier in the study, we established:

- God does not lie

- God does not change

- God fulfills what He speaks

If God declares a promise in specific terms:

- And those terms are later redefined

Then the original statement:

Did not mean what it appeared to mean

The Broader Theological Impact

This issue extends beyond Israel.

If specific promises can be reinterpreted:

- Any promise could be reinterpreted

- Assurance becomes uncertain

- Language loses stability

Final Logical Structure

If:

- God gives specific, measurable promises

- God fulfills similar promises literally in the past

- Scripture does not redefine those promises

Then:

Those promises must be fulfilled as originally stated

Final Thoughts on Rebuttal 2

The claim that Israel's promises are fulfilled spiritually in the Church requires a shift in interpretation that is not supported by the text of scripture. The promises themselves are presented in concrete, measurable terms, and the established pattern of prophetic fulfillment demonstrates that such language is to be understood literally. Because no explicit redefinition is given, and because applying a symbolic interpretation introduces inconsistency into the handling of scripture, the conclusion must be that these promises remain as originally stated and await literal fulfillment. Therefore, the spiritualization of Israel's promises does not arise from the text itself, but from an external interpretive system imposed upon it.

Rebuttal 3 — "Israel Failed, Therefore the Promises Were Forfeited"

This argument is one of the most persuasive on the surface because it appeals to a principle that appears reasonable:

- Israel was disobedient

- Israel broke the Law

- Therefore, Israel lost its covenantal standing

From this perspective, replacement theology presents itself not as an arbitrary system, but as a logical consequence of Israel's failure.

However, the validity of this argument depends on a critical assumption:

That the promises made to Israel were conditional upon Israel's obedience

If this assumption is not supported by scripture, then the conclusion collapses.

The Need to Distinguish Between Covenants

The first step in evaluating this claim is to distinguish between two types of covenants found in scripture:

1. **Conditional covenants** — dependent on obedience

2. **Unconditional covenants** — dependent on God's promise

The confusion often arises when these two are blended together.

The Mosaic Covenant (Conditional)

The Law given through Moses clearly operates on a conditional basis:

- Blessing for obedience

- Judgment for disobedience

Deuteronomy 28:1–2

"If thou shalt hearken diligently… all these blessings shall come on thee…"

Deuteronomy 28:15

"If thou wilt not hearken… all these curses shall come upon thee…"

Observation

The Mosaic system is clearly:

Performance-based

The Abrahamic Covenant (Unconditional)

In contrast, the covenant made with Abraham operates differently.

Genesis 15:18

"Unto thy seed have I given this land…"

In Genesis 15, the covenant is ratified in a way that is critically important:

- God alone passes between the pieces

- Abraham does not

Meaning

The covenant is:

Unilateral—dependent on God alone

The New Testament Clarifies This Distinction

Galatians 3:17

"The covenant... the law... cannot disannul, that it should make the promise of none effect."

Observation

- The Law came later

- The Law does not cancel the promise

Therefore:

Israel's failure under the Law:

Does not nullify the earlier covenant

The Ongoing Status of Israel Despite Unbelief

The New Testament directly addresses Israel's condition.

Romans 11:28

"As concerning the gospel, they are enemies... but as touching the election, they are beloved..."

Observation

Israel is described in two ways simultaneously:

- Enemies (in current unbelief)

- Beloved (in covenantal standing)

Romans 11:29

"For the gifts and calling of God are without repentance."

Observation

- "Without repentance" means:
  - Not revoked
  - Not withdrawn
  - Not reversed

Meaning

God's calling of Israel:

Remains in effect regardless of their current condition

The Logical Breakdown of the "Forfeiture" Argument

Let us examine the claim logically:

If Israel's failure cancels the promise:

- Then the promise was conditional
- But scripture defines the Abrahamic covenant as unconditional

If the promise is unconditional:

- It cannot be canceled by human failure

Therefore:

The argument collapses at its foundation.

The Pattern of Discipline Without Cancellation

Scripture consistently shows:

- Israel is judged

- Israel is scattered

- Israel suffers consequences

But:

- Israel is never permanently rejected

This pattern has already been established:

- Correction → yes

- Destruction → no

- Cancellation → no

The Deeper Theological Issue

If failure cancels God's promises:

- No covenant can stand

- No promise is secure

This would affect:

- Abrahamic covenant

- Davidic covenant

- New Covenant

And ultimately:

- All confidence in God's word

Connection to God's Character

Earlier we established:

- God does not change

- God does not lie

- God fulfills what He declares

If God cancels an unconditional promise due to human failure:

- The promise was not unconditional

- The declaration was not fixed

This creates a contradiction

The Proper Conclusion

Israel's failure:

- Explains their discipline

- Explains their scattering

- Explains their temporary condition

But it does not:

- Cancel their identity

- Transfer their promises

- End their role

Final Thoughts on Rebuttal 3

The claim that Israel forfeited its promises due to disobedience rests on a misunderstanding of the nature of God's covenants. While the Mosaic covenant operated on a conditional basis and resulted in judgment when broken, the Abrahamic covenant was established as an unconditional promise grounded in God's own commitment. The New Testament explicitly affirms that this covenant cannot be annulled and that God's calling remains in effect despite Israel's current unbelief. Therefore, Israel's failure results in discipline, not cancellation, and the promises made to them remain intact and await fulfillment.

Rebuttal 4 — "There Is Only One People of God"

The claim that there is only one people of God is often used to support the idea that Israel and the Church are not distinct, but are instead the same entity viewed from different perspectives.

From this, it is concluded that:

- Israel has no continuing distinct role

- The Church has absorbed or fulfilled Israel's identity

- All promises now apply to a single unified group sometimes referred to as The New Israel of God

At first glance, this argument appears to align with the unity described in the New Testament. However, its validity depends on a critical assumption:

That unity eliminates distinction

Clarifying the Nature of Unity in Scripture

Scripture clearly teaches unity among believers.

Galatians 3:28

"There is neither Jew nor Greek… for ye are all one in Christ Jesus."

Observation

This verse emphasizes:

- Equality in salvation

- Unity in Christ

Important Question

Does this verse mean:

- All distinctions cease to exist?or

- All distinctions cease to determine salvation?

The context answers this:

It is addressing:

Access to salvation—not identity categories

Distinctions Still Recognized After Salvation

Even after establishing unity in Christ, scripture continues to recognize distinctions.

1 Corinthians 10:32

"Give none offence, neither to the Jews, nor to the Gentiles, nor to the church of God:"

Observation

Three distinct groups are identified:

1. Jews

2. Gentiles

3. Church

This is significant

This statement is written:

- After the establishment of the Church

- After the inclusion of Gentiles

Yet the distinctions remain.

The Meaning of "One New Man"

Ephesians 2:14–15

"For he is our peace, who hath made both one… To make in himself of twain one new man…"

Observations

- Two groups exist:
    - Jews
    - Gentiles
- A new entity is formed:
    - "One new man"

Key Insight

The text does not say:

- The two groups become identical

It says:

A new entity is formed from both

The Difference Between Unity and Identity

Unity means:

- Shared salvation
- Shared standing before God
- Shared participation in Christ

Identity means:

- Origin

- Covenant role

- National distinction

These are not the same thing

The Logical Problem with the Claim

If unity eliminates distinction:

- Jew would no longer exist as a category

- Gentile would no longer exist as a category

But scripture continues to use these categories

Therefore:

Unity does not erase identity

The Ongoing Distinction in Prophecy

Throughout prophetic scripture:

- Israel is addressed as Israel

- Nations are addressed as nations

- Roles remain distinct

This continues even into future contexts:

- Israel repents as a nation

- Nations interact with Israel

The Consequence of Collapsing the Distinction

If Israel and the Church are made identical:

- National promises lose meaning

- Covenant structure collapses

- Prophetic clarity is lost

The result is:

A system where:

- Everything becomes generalized

- Specific promises lose definition

The Proper Understanding

Scripture presents:

- One way of salvation

- One body in Christ

But within that unity:

- Distinct roles remain

- Distinct identities remain

- Distinct covenant relationships remain

Connection to the Broader Study

This aligns with:

- Romans 11 → Israel distinct but temporarily hardened

- Galatians 3 → unity in blessing, not identity transfer

- Covenants → still tied to Israel

Final Thoughts on Rebuttal 4

The claim that there is only one people of God becomes misleading when it is used to eliminate distinctions that scripture continues to maintain. While the New Testament clearly teaches unity in Christ and equality in salvation, it does not erase the distinctions between Israel and the Church. Instead, it presents a unified body composed of distinct groups, each retaining its identity and role within God's broader plan. Therefore, unity does not imply replacement, and the existence of one people of God in a spiritual sense does not negate the continued distinction and future role of Israel as a nation or a people.

Rebuttal 5 — "The Kingdom Is Only Spiritual"

The claim that the kingdom is purely spiritual is often presented as a refinement of biblical teaching rather than a contradiction of it. It acknowledges that God reigns, that Christ is King, and that believers participate in that reign—but it denies that this kingdom involves a literal restoration of Israel, a geographic center, or a visible rule over nations.

According to this view:

- The kingdom is internal, not external

- Spiritual, not political or national

- Present in the hearts of believers rather than expressed in a future earthly structure

At first glance, this seems to align with certain New Testament passages. However, the question is not whether the kingdom has a spiritual dimension—it clearly does.

The question is:

Does scripture limit the kingdom to a spiritual reality, or does it present both spiritual and literal aspects?

The Expectation of the Apostles After the Resurrection

The clearest place to begin is after the resurrection of Christ, when the apostles had received direct teaching concerning the kingdom.

Acts 1:6

"Lord, wilt thou at this time restore again the kingdom to Israel?"

Observation

This question reveals several key assumptions:

- The kingdom is expected to be restored
- The restoration is connected to Israel
- The expectation is future

This is not an early misunderstanding. This occurs:

- After the resurrection
- After extended teaching

Acts 1:3

"Being seen of them forty days, and speaking of the things pertaining to the kingdom of God:"

Meaning

The apostles' understanding of the kingdom was shaped by Christ Himself.

The Response of Christ

Acts 1:7

"It is not for you to know the times or the seasons…"

Critical Observation

Christ does not say:

- "The kingdom will not be restored"
- "The kingdom is only spiritual"
- "Israel is no longer relevant"

He addresses only:

Timing

This distinction is decisive

He corrects:

- When

He does not correct:

- What

- Who

The Old Testament Description of the Kingdom

To understand what the apostles expected, we must examine how the kingdom is described in the Old Testament.

Isaiah 2:2–3

"All nations shall flow unto it… For out of Zion shall go forth the law, and the word of the Lord from Jerusalem."

Observations

- There is a central location:
    - Zion / Jerusalem
- There are nations:
    - Flowing toward that location
- There is governance:
    - Law proceeding outward

Zechariah 14:9

"And the Lord shall be king over all the earth…"

Observation

- The reign is:
    - Global
    - Visible
    - Over the earth

The Structural Elements of the Kingdom

From these passages, the kingdom includes:

- A King (the Lord)

- A location (Jerusalem)

- A people (Israel)

- Nations (distinct and interacting)

- Governance (law proceeding outward)

These are not abstract elements

They describe:

A structured, observable kingdom

The Problem with a Purely Spiritual Interpretation

If the kingdom is only spiritual:

- Geographic references lose their meaning

- National distinctions become irrelevant

- Prophetic descriptions become symbolic and unreliable

This creates a disconnect

Between:

- What the text describes and

- What the interpretation allows

The Present vs Future Aspect of the Kingdom

Scripture does teach that:

- The kingdom has a present aspect

- God reigns now

However, it also teaches:

- A future manifestation

- A visible reign

- A restored order

These are not contradictory

They are:

Complementary

The Logical Issue

If the kingdom is redefined as spiritual only:

- The apostles misunderstood it

- The prophets described it incorrectly

- The text must be reinterpreted

But none of these are stated in scripture

The Consistent Conclusion

The kingdom includes:

- A present spiritual reality

- A future literal fulfillment

It is not:

- One or the other

It is:

Both

Connection to the Broader Argument

This aligns with:

- Acts 1 → expectation not corrected

- Prophets → literal descriptions

- Covenants → national promises

- Revelation → structured future events

Conclusion of Rebuttal 5

The claim that the kingdom is purely spiritual cannot account for the full range of scriptural descriptions. While the kingdom does include a present spiritual dimension, it is also consistently presented as a future, literal, and structured reality involving a restored Israel, a central location in Jerusalem, and the governance of nations under the reign of Christ. Because Christ did not correct the apostles' expectation of such a kingdom, and because the prophets describe it in concrete terms, the conclusion must be that the kingdom is not limited to a spiritual interpretation but includes a literal fulfillment consistent with the language in which it is revealed. If a literal interpretation is not to be taken from the text, the apostles were done a disservice by not being corrected in their understanding before being sent out to teach the world the truth in Christ Jesus.

Rebuttal 6 — "Believers Are the Seed of Abraham, Therefore the Church Is Israel"

This argument is rooted primarily in Galatians 3 and is often presented as decisive proof that the Church has inherited Israel's identity.

The reasoning typically follows this progression:

1. Believers are called the seed of Abraham

2. Israel is the seed of Abraham

3. Therefore, believers are Israel

At first glance, this appears to be a straightforward syllogism. However, the validity of the conclusion depends entirely on how the term **"seed of Abraham"** is being used in the passage.

The Immediate Context of Galatians 3

Before defining the term, we must identify the subject of the chapter.

Galatians 3:6

"Even as Abraham believed God, and it was accounted to him for righteousness."

Observation

The chapter is focused on:

- Justification by faith

- Not national identity

This is reinforced in the following verse:

Galatians 3:7

"They which are of faith, the same are the children of Abraham."

Key Point

"Children of Abraham" here is defined in terms of:

Faith, not ethnicity

The Promise Being Referenced

Galatians 3:8

"In thee shall all nations be blessed."

Observation

This refers to the **blessing aspect** of the Abrahamic covenant:

- Salvation

- Justification

- Inclusion of the Gentiles

Important Distinction

This is not:

- The land promise

- The national promise

- The kingdom structure

The Central Focus: Christ as the Seed

Galatians 3:16

"Now to Abraham and his seed were the promises made… not… to seeds, as of many; but… to thy seed, which is Christ."

Observation

Paul identifies the ultimate "seed" as:

- Jesus Christ

Meaning

The promise flows through:

Christ as the singular, central seed

What It Means to Be "Abraham's Seed"

Galatians 3:29

"If ye be Christ's, then are ye Abraham's seed, and heirs according to the promise."

Observation

Believers become Abraham's seed by:

- Being in Christ

Therefore the relationship is:

Christ → Abraham → Believers

The Critical Distinction

At this point, we must distinguish between two uses of "seed" in scripture:

1. Physical/National Seed

- Refers to Israel
- Connected to:
  - Land
  - Nation
  - Covenant identity

2. Spiritual Seed

- Refers to believers
- Connected to:
  - Faith
  - Justification
  - Blessing

The Error in the Replacement Argument

The argument assumes:

- That these two meanings are identical

But they are not

They are:

Related—but distinct

Supporting Clarification from Romans

Romans 4:11–12

"The father of all them that believe... And the father of circumcision..."

Observation

Abraham is:

- Father of believing Gentiles

- Father of Israel

Meaning

Two relationships exist simultaneously:

- Spiritual

- National

Why This Matters

If being Abraham's seed spiritually means becoming Israel nationally:

- The distinction between Israel and Gentiles disappears

- National promises must be reassigned

But scripture never makes that step

Connection to the Broader Framework

This aligns with:

- Romans 11 → Gentiles grafted in, not replacing

- Ephesians 2 → one new man, not identity transfer

- Covenants → still tied to Israel

The Logical Conclusion

If:

- Christ is the central seed

- Believers are connected to Christ

- Israel remains a defined nation

Then:

Participation in Abraham's blessing does not equal replacement of Israel's identity

---

Final Thoughts on Rebuttal 6

Galatians 3 teaches that all who are in Christ share in the spiritual blessings promised to Abraham, becoming his seed in the sense of faith and inheritance through Christ. However, the passage does not redefine Israel as a nation, nor does it transfer the land, kingdom, or covenantal identity to the Church. The focus of the chapter is justification and inclusion in blessing, not the reassignment of national promises. Therefore, while believers are rightly called Abraham's seed in a spiritual sense, this does not equate the Church with Israel or support the conclusion that Israel's distinct role has been replaced.

Rebuttal 7 — "The Israel of God Is the Church"

This argument is built primarily on a single phrase found in Galatians 6:16, where Paul writes:

"And as many as walk according to this rule, peace be on them, and mercy, and upon the Israel of God."

From this statement, it is often concluded that:

- "The Israel of God" is a title for the Church

- Israel is therefore redefined as the community of believers

- The distinction between Israel and the Church is removed

At first glance, this may seem plausible. However, careful examination of the text reveals that this conclusion depends on assumptions that are not required by the passage itself.

To properly understand this verse, we must examine:

1. The immediate context

2. The grammatical structure

3. Paul's consistent use of the term "Israel"

4. The broader theological framework

The Immediate Context of the Passage

The closing section of Galatians is not focused on defining national identity. Instead, it addresses the contrast between:

- Flesh and Spirit

- External religious markers and internal transformation

Galatians 6:15

"For in Christ Jesus neither circumcision availeth any thing, nor uncircumcision, but a new creature."

Observation

The focus is:

- Spiritual condition

- New creation

Important Clarification

This passage is addressing:

How one is accepted before God—not who replaces whom

The Structure of Galatians 6:16

Now we return to the verse itself:

"Peace be on them, and mercy, and upon the Israel of God."

Key Question

Is Paul describing:

- One group (the Church = Israel)? or

- Two related but distinct groups?

The Role of the Conjunction "And"

The verse includes the conjunction:

"and"

In normal grammatical usage, "and" indicates:

- Addition

- Distinction

- Continuation

It does not normally indicate:

- Definition

- Replacement

- Identity equivalence

The Most Natural Reading of the Text

The verse can be read as:

- "Peace be on them" → those walking according to the rule (believers generally)

- "And upon the Israel of God" → a second group being specifically included

This results in:

Two groups being addressed:

1. Believers broadly

2. The Israel of God (believing Israel)

Paul's Consistent Use of the Term "Israel"

To determine whether Paul is redefining Israel here, we must examine how he uses the term elsewhere.

Romans 9:4

"Who are Israelites; to whom pertaineth the adoption, and the glory, and the covenants…"

Romans 11:1

"For I also am an Israelite…"

Observation

In every clear instance:

- "Israel" refers to:
    - The ethnic/national people

There is no clear case where Paul redefines "Israel" as the Church

---

The Problem of Doctrinal Weight

If Galatians 6:16 were redefining Israel, it would be:

- A major theological shift
- A foundational doctrinal statement

But the verse appears:

- In a closing blessing
- Without explanation
- Without development

This creates a tension

Major doctrinal changes in scripture are:

- Clearly explained
- Repeated
- Systematically developed

This is not.

The Logical Problem with the Replacement Reading

If "Israel of God" = Church:

- Paul introduces a completely new definition
- Without explanation
- Without precedent
- Without support elsewhere

This would contradict:

- His consistent use of the term
- His extended arguments in Romans 9–11

The Consistent Alternative

The passage fits naturally if understood as:

- A blessing on believers
- With a specific inclusion of believing Israel

This interpretation:

- Requires no redefinition
- Aligns with Paul's usage

- Maintains distinction

Connection to the Broader Framework

This aligns with:

- Romans 11 → Israel remains distinct

- 1 Corinthians 10:32 → categories remain

- Ephesians 2 → unity without identity loss

The Logical Conclusion

If:

- "Israel" consistently refers to national Israel

- The grammar suggests addition

- No redefinition is given

Then:

"The Israel of God" is best understood as believing Israel—not the Church as a whole

---

Final Thoughts on Rebuttal 7

Galatians 6:16 does not provide a sufficient basis for redefining Israel as the Church. The grammatical structure of the verse supports the understanding of two groups rather than one, and Paul's consistent use of the term "Israel" throughout his writings refers to the ethnic and national people to whom the covenants were originally given. Because the statement appears in a closing blessing without doctrinal explanation, it cannot reasonably be treated as a foundational redefinition of Israel's identity. Therefore, the phrase "the Israel of God" is most naturally understood as referring to believing Israelites, maintaining the distinction upheld throughout scripture rather than collapsing it into a single category.

PART XXII — FINAL SYNTHESIS AND CONCLUSION

The Purpose of This Final Section

From the beginning, this study has followed a consistent method:

To allow scripture to define its own terms, establish its own structures, and reach its own conclusions without reinterpretation.

The goal has not been to:

- Force a system onto the text

- Select isolated passages

- Build a conclusion from assumption

Instead, the goal has been:

To follow each line of scriptural evidence wherever it leads—and then examine where those lines converge

The Nature of the Argument Presented

No single section in this study stands alone.

Each addresses a different category:

- Covenants

- Identity

- Distinction

- Prophetic structure

- Historical alignment

- The character of God

- Interpretive consistency

Each category has been examined independently.

And yet, something consistent has occurred:

Each line of reasoning—when followed carefully—arrives at the same conclusion.

They do not diverge.

They:

Converge

The Covenantal Foundation

The study began by establishing that:

- The promises made to Abraham are unconditional and grounded in God's own Character

- They were confirmed by an oath

- They are not annulled by the Law

These promises include:

- A people

- A land

- A future blessing

Because they are:

- Rooted in God's oath

- Grounded in His character

They cannot be revoked, reassigned, or redefined

The Identity of Israel

Scripture consistently defines Israel as:

- A nation

- A people descended from Abraham

- A group with a specific covenantal role

- A group chosen by God Himself as His people

This identity is:

- Maintained through judgment

- Preserved through scattering

- Never reassigned

Israel remains Israel

The Distinction Between Israel and the Church

The New Testament introduces the Church as:

- A new body

- Composed of both Jews and Gentiles

- United in Christ

However, unity is not presented as identity replacement.

Scripture maintains:

- Distinction in origin

- Distinction in role

- Distinction in prophetic function

The Church does not replace Israel—it exists alongside it within God's plan

---

The Present Condition of Israel

Israel is described as:

- Partially hardened

- Temporarily blinded

Romans 11:25

"Blindness in part… until the fullness of the Gentiles…"

The key word:

"Until"

Meaning

Israel's present condition is:

- Real

- But temporary

The Future Restoration of Israel

Scripture consistently points to:

- A future repentance

- A national restoration

- A renewed role in the kingdom

This includes:

- Regathering to the land

- Recognition of the Messiah

- Participation in the kingdom

These events have not yet been fully realized

The Structure of the Kingdom

The kingdom is described as:

- Ruled by Christ

- Centered in Jerusalem

- Involving nations

- Structured and observable

It includes:

- A present spiritual aspect

- A future literal fulfillment

Both dimensions exist together

The Consistency of Prophetic Fulfillment

Prophecy throughout scripture demonstrates:

- Specific language

- Literal fulfillment

This pattern is consistent:

- In the first coming of Christ

- In the unfolding of historical events

Therefore

Future prophecy must be understood in the same way

The Character of God

Underlying every section is a single foundation:

- God does not change

- God does not lie

- God fulfills what He speaks

Malachi 3:6

"I change not..."

Therefore

His promises:

- Remain fixed

- Remain reliable

- Remain as declared

The Historical Alignment

History reflects the pattern described in scripture:

- Israel was scattered

- Israel was preserved

- Israel has been regathered (in part)

The process is not complete—but it is clearly in motion

The Rebuttal Section Confirmed

Every major argument for replacement theology was examined:

- Church as Israel

- Spiritualized promises

- Israel's failure

- Unity removing distinction

- Spiritual-only kingdom

- Abraham's seed argument

- "Israel of God"

Each was found to require:

- Reinterpretation of clear language

- Inconsistency in method

- Assumptions not stated in the text

The Final Logical Structure

If:

- God made unconditional promises

- God confirmed them with an oath

- God does not change

- Israel remains defined in scripture

- Israel's future is clearly described

- That future has not yet occurred

Then:

Those promises must still be fulfilled as given

The Final Theological Conclusion

Scripture presents a unified and consistent framework in which Israel remains a distinct, covenantal nation with promises that are unconditional, ongoing, and not yet fully realized. The Church is introduced as a new body composed of both Jews and Gentiles, sharing in spiritual blessings without replacing Israel's national identity or covenantal role. Israel's present condition is temporary and purposeful, leading toward a future restoration that fulfills the promises made by God. The prophetic scriptures, the teachings of Christ, the writings of the apostles, and the observable patterns of history all align in maintaining this distinction and pointing toward a literal fulfillment of God's covenantal commitments. Therefore, when the full testimony of scripture is allowed to stand without reinterpretation, the conclusion is clear: God is not finished with Israel, and the concept of replacement theology does not align with the consistent message of scripture.